It's About Time

The Manifesto of Spiritual Communism

HOWARD VENZE

IT'S ABOUT TIME

2016 Fluid Luhancy Press Trade Paperback Edition

Published in the United States of America.

ISBN-13: 978-0692705391

ISBN-10: 0692705392

Library of Congress Control Number: 2016907753

HowardVenze.com

LOS ANGELES, CA

SPECIAL THANKS TO LINDA GARBETT

"How did it get so late so soon?"
~ Dr. Seuss

It's About Time

We do not see the world directly.

We see through our eyes. think of someone looking up through a periscope. They see what the periscope lets them see.

There is no free will yet
the future is not determined. variables alter.

a choice might be an option. a choice opens the door to more choice. all the choices are predetermined but if the predetermination leads you to more options leading to even more choices, it does not bring about a conclusion. so it is not causal. It leads to more options. It is opening the door into more choice, a bigger universe of facts to consider, not less.

You can't write an equation to cover the infinite variables.

Knowing the original conditions will not lead to predicting everything which happens later. Likewise, if we look back at what happened, we do not see all the things we did not see or could have done. We only see the things we can see we did not see or did not do. Which means much of life is forgettable and has no meaning.

What is meaning?

Who are we?

We are our long-term memory. Our short-term memory is our activity. What is linked between the two is meaningful. It is meaningful enough that you remembered it.

There is nothing which people say except for that which is a product of memory. It may be spontaneous. If the memory does not remember the spontaneous, it will not be registered as realization. Realization is a learned conscious act. To be timeless requires no learning, memory, or conscious act. it is the bliss that most people crave.

If people remember a spontaneous act, they remember the memory, not the spontaneity unless they are connected. If you are connected to your memories you are living them.

Everything we experience is our short-term memory. Our experience is a memory of what we experience.

If you think about who we are as people, we are the memory of ourselves, with all its ideas, assumptions, conclusions, etc.

as the spirit of the thing, we are more instantaneous.

Schopenhauer had a problem with life. He saw it in terms of will, which influenced Nietzsche.

Life lives according to its nature, not its will. People think in terms of willing or force when nature contains yang and yin. it is both what you thought it is and what you didn't think it is.

to will or to see the world in terms of force is to see only part of the picture. there is the rest of the picture to see. that is the part you do not have to see in order to see it.

The mind puts together an image.

Our experience is what happens to us. it is our version. it's put together. What we experience is what our mind put together and arranged for us to see. It is our idea of what happened. We know nothing more of what we experience than our experience. We experience a memory that has been self-edited to enable us to view what occurred, in order for us to put together an idea of what happened.

We are trained to respond to stimuli. We learn to feel and recognize the sensation.

We have a noisy society. noisy + dumb. too busy to see.

What is real? What is real is this little life we have, not some ideal truth, not an "eternal" truth.

Eternity is timeless. Our life is fleeting. The reality of Life exists in Time. the reality of our lives are what we make of them. the truth is we can start off happy rather than impoverished. rather than sinners, beggars, charlatans or fools.

We want to be happy. Happiness is something familiar, not mysterious, not beyond knowing. Happiness is not something we do not know.

paths do work and meditation techniques do work. that being said; People are sitting there to gain something. if they aren't they are wasting their time. if they are they are wasting their time.

Waiting will (probably) not get it.

Patience will (probably) not get it. Only to be cosmically informed that Happiness or Wonder is what you consist of. it is your nature. What you are made out of is cosmic stuff, satchitananda.

this existence we have already is satchitananda, but our society has translated the meaning of life to be samsara. The importance of life we attach to is Samsara. We exist as the rat on the wheel of existentially being in time. We feel life to be stress.

A path is not needed, but if we enter a path let us get the right path. To consider anything, to start a spiritual path or to meditate is to start with the assumptions of those who thought there was a reason to enter a path or meditate. something to get or do, or why do it? there is a reason to do what we do. to start a path is to see a distance between the divine and ourselves. or to see this as a journey within the divine.

There are rules and ongoing conditions, which must be mastered to go on. Much of the spiritual search is an attempt to get back to original conditions, before we were here to stink up the place. but we are here. the way is not to accept things as they are.

People in general think free will means you are free to do what you would like to do. You are free, people think. If you are spiritually liberated your mind is thinking of what is appropriate for it to think. it is not free to be free. People confuse a mind on holiday with a freely employed mind.

The biological system does not like to waste energy. People tend to think of free will as the right to do something different than what they are doing now. They think of being free to pursue other options rather than being free as they are.

We gather information. We hear and see at certain speeds and what reaches us travels at certain speeds. this sounds obvious but there is more to it. Our mind is a nest. Information, which is traveling at a certain speed to reach us is received and decoded into our looking speed, out time of viewing. Our "mind's eye", we could say it is an imaging machine, it is timeless, but it ascribes time accordingly in the order received to make sense of things, and that lets us do something about what it is we'd like to do or think we need to do.

Our viewing gives us a bias. Our unseen bias is that viewing ascribes location to things from our point of view. Because our eyes are shaped we see a certain way. To look at an eye is to see a roundish object, but to look through an eye gives shape to how we see because we are viewing as if in a tunnel from back --> forward gives us a sense of direction and we order the sensing of our environment as time. Our perceiving instills a sense of time as it is viewed in sequence.

The Medium is the Massage

As McLuhan says, the media through which we perceive shapes our perception.

the fact we are set up to view in a certain way; the reception combined with the fact we walk back + forth, forwards, sideways + backwards gives us ordering. the ordering of perception, which is time, is done in the perceiving as well as the perceived. This is important because if people want a sense of the eternal, to know they are beyond death, it lies beneath their ordering of time, in their perception of time, not in the future.

Robert De Niro said to the cross-eyed drunk, "You looking at me?"

I want to simplify things. Teachings are to establish rules. Rules concern functioning. Where to judge is in how well the system functions, not how the system stays true to a rulebook. The rulebook is about rules of the system. The book might contain more than how much someone reads into it, or the book might contain less than what someone reads into it.

Rules + laws are meant to be followed. This means everyone must understand the rules in order to follow the rules. If a rule is saying one thing no one needs to read into the rule more than what the rule says on the surface. There is no reason to read more into a rule than what the rule says.

Ideally, there is no reason for law schools. If a school is needed to understand and practice the law, which we must all obey on a daily basis, it is too complicated. The law should be no more complicated than the 7th grade, or we the people will not be able to comprehend it, that is, we cannot obey if we cannot comprehend.

Civil or criminal law must be simple. Business law concerning contracts could easily be simple, meaning transparent, that is, written in language people understand. If a contract is written clearly it may be understood. If it is written as contracts are, we need lawyers to give us their interpretation.

The bible is simple: Be honest. Be responsible. we need good directions. Stage magic is about misdirection. Stage magic is entertaining for a period of time but then it gets boring. We want the real thing. To arrive at our destination we need good directions, which like the law, must be simple enough for us to understand.

The first story of the bible is one common to our time; the lie (the problem or situation) and the cover up. My suggestion, don't moralize at first. Don't fall for the misdirection. At first see what is happening. The problem with Adam and Eve is not eating the apple or being "bad." The problem is after they got caught and God is present they feared God and covered up as if they could fool God. They were evasive. They could not understand the loving kindness of God due to their feelings of guilt, so the story is reduced to a story of guilt, not redemption.

The second story is Cain + Abel. This is a similar story. Cain is evasive. We humans fall for the misdirection. We listen to the evasive words of Cain as if they warrant believing. He questions whether he is his brother's keeper and we take the message or meaning to be we should be moral. We make morality an issue when the issue is honesty and evasiveness. If you are honest you can be moral. If you are not honest you cannot be moral. A psychotic knows what is right + wrong, they just do not care. Hypocrites live in limbo. They think to themselves they do care but it is a fallacy, they are hypocrites. you see it or you don't.

It is amazing how long it takes some people to learn, to regain trust admit the truth. Apologize if an apology is needed and live a life in which we don't backtrack and lie. To continue to deceive. it gets harder to earn trust after a while and for good reason.

We have laws. Laws are what we are responsible for. That is the established code of behavior. We should look to the law for what is the ordered or permissible behavior. If we think what is moral is so important that it needs to be followed then it becomes a law thru the process that society uses to make laws. People do not need to refer to a bible or a God to know what is right or wrong. If we have to refer to something else than what is appearing in a situation, a "Higher Code," as to what is right and wrong, it is too complicated. Ethics, like Morality is nuance or finesse. Morality as seen thru Plato and Socrates becomes the enemy of the real, of what is really the case.

Knowing is Memory

My view on evolutionary biology: To evolve takes time. To live in time as an animal requires one to eat with the possibility of being eaten. Living has always involved an element of fear. The fear is of the future. It's anticipatory. It involves time. To be time-less is the end of evolution. The end of fear. the end of anxiety.

this is peace. this is love. this is god.

god is peace is love.

god is peace is love is known when we are free of fear.

when we are free of anxiety.

words are not needed.

To be mature is to have perceived time + the lessons of time, whether you know it or not. Maturity involves moving onto a more nuanced level of understanding. It lives life in more of its totality because it can see more.

If you can see there are two sides to the story --> you can see there are more than two sides. There is a disagreement. That is the third side; the fact of the mismatch.

There is not another truth out there.

How did the self-important tho populous writer refer to himself? We the people.

philosophy: Wittgenstein says, "Whereof one cannot speak, thereof one must be silent." Poetic yes, but what does it say? does it say it is impossible to say some things, or is there a range in which we may speak? speaking is like the game of horseshoes, close enough might do the job..

What Wittgenstein says he can say, he can say. What a mystic can say is also said and understood. Do words serve to mystify, clarify, or both? The problem is not in the saying, it is in the understanding; what got us here and why are we doing what we are doing.

Wittgenstein's brilliance is like the Dark Ages, something taken as real but isn't. To hear Wittgenstein's famous line, Whereof, is to think he is describing a proper encounter with the ineffable, but frankly speaking, Wittgenstein's rules of thinking and speaking allowed him very little of importance to say, as for him most everything is not capable of being discussed with words. He correctly says what is most important in his work is what is not written.

Growing up I did not hear the phrase, "be still and know I am God." Growing up I thought only Moses met and got to know God. It seemed forbidden in Judaism while Yoga suggested i could meet the dude. Our basic framework for understanding the nature of things is we work and get a day off. On the off day we can rest. God exists throughout the entire cycle, but the basic idea is when the work is done you can have peace of mind. and this is what God is as well as where God is known.

Essentially, God is not about command and control. That is only when necessary.

Time is a measure of the passage of one object compared or relative to another object. You can compare yourself with another you to say you aged, but you do not move relative to yourself. You do not measure time within yourself. Time is compared to something else. You are timeless. You are ageless within yourself. Compared to something else you age. I do not feel like I age. My understanding changes. I feel like I am the same. I am what I am.

questioning my reality: To be or not to be? which is to say, do I exist?

It seems silly. Of course I exist. We could open up the question for further examination. At times it seems I as a separate individual have no existence. Also the experience could be described as empty or still or void, still any description would require one to respond to an enquiry and use words. This would not tell the whole story, unless something clicks between the ears of the listener.

If Society understood the bible stories we wouldn't need God. Things would run well and we would have enough love. We would not be lacking. God is found within, meaning that God is within conditions; not in our inner mind, not within our inner soul, and not in our private self. God is a name for the experience when the truth is revealed. It is a realization you are privileged to get and understand. The significance is known. It does not have to be extraterrestrial. It does not have to explain. It is understood more in coming to terms with yourself.

When a life is saved we realize it is precious. God comes to mind. We call in God to thank. We understand the specialness. This specialness has something more to it than can be reduced to mechanics or a soul-less life but life becomes mundane. Samsara is nothing other than life, which has become mundane. Nirvana is nothing else than peace of mind.

There is no other soul than us. The foundation for us being here are these bodies. We think because we have brains. Our sense of self is our soul. We do not have a soul. A soul is another name for a person and there is something special or divine about being a person. (despite how hellish it is to be a person.)

An atheist or a empiricist may wish to explain away our sense of God, divinity, and holiness. Do they think their feelings of love can be explained strictly by explaining them as hormones and nerves? Are they satisfied with the explanation being a substitute for the real thing? The explanation is a sign. It is not the location.

God is something people sense. You either get it or you are deficient in your understanding. You lack a sense of what is Truly profound. People believe in God for real reasons.

It's like saying the taste of something is part of why we eat food. We need food for energy and material as well. There is something silly about reducing the experience of eating to a physiological explanation or to say taste does not exist. It shows inadequacy, a need to bring this down to a level you know.

It's when the questioning is over that a sense of peace of mind comes about. This is what many of us are calling God. There is no need to call this God, but this is what people are calling God.

in so many ways, to say it is God is not to say anything at all. If it makes an atheist happy to call this No God, be happy. A mystic might call God no idea, so no God.

To say if there is a God or not will not change things. There is no reason to put a name on what people are calling God. However, it is normal to refer to something with a name. Some people find God in some activity. Maybe God is just a metaphor, but a metaphor for what, itself? (even if it is just hope + longing and that is pathetic, there is something in the actual drive of hope + longing which is the sense of God. Likewise, there is something so pathetic in thinking a human's explanation is at a level of understanding to make the final decision as to whether there is a God or not. Once we humans come up with a Grand Theory for Everything, when quantum mechanics can be joined with relativity theory and we humans can explain everything, honestly, you have to say we are not yet in a position to deny God. Yes, many or most people's ideas of God are childish. That does not dismiss the proposition.

To be enlightened is to be introduced to your Self and we already happen to be our Self. Our body based psychological selves that we live everyday, this too is the Self, but conditions must be close enough to jog your memory.

The Snake in the Garden of Eden story is the tongue. The tongue tasted and speaks of the apple. The words convinced and the words got the blame.

Who are we? We are runts. We would stick out our tongue to tell of our dislike and point with our finger to indicate a direction but we've grown up, we've been civilized. We use words to get our point across.

What was known as a gesture is confused by saying it in the long form:- formalized communication using words.

Realization is getting the answer. The mind has formulated some question. It wonders. What I wanted was something cosmically brilliant. NOT to go back to original conditions, but to know. The grace is to reveal. You cannot turn the fundamental fact of this into something else. You cannot transcend your Self, only your stuff, but Humanity thru no fault of its own has turned the natural life into Samsara. Samsara is looking to provide, getting the bucks, being afraid, based in time and never getting a lasting satisfaction. Our economic model is based on our view of evolutionary biology. Satisfaction is not in the interest of Samsara. We must always be looking for what is next. We hunt and gather. There are limited supplies and life is uncertain. Anxiously we twist in the winds of whim.

Knowledge, Education is the gift we have been given to rise above the uncertainties of life, to face life with calmness in the face of uncertainty. Enlightenment or God is not to know everything before hand. Would God bother to know the future? There is no time. What's to be known from God's point of view? Not much. Let things run themselves. This is how much God loves us. God loves us enough to trust us as adults, not to send his only son to save us.

Why God? based in time it is natural to be afraid and hope things will work out. Evolutionary biologists look to biology for reasonable explanations for behavior. I run into the wall of cognitive dissonance. For biologists to maintain their faith biology must behave rationally with reasonable or explainable reasons, as Nature is so reasonable. Why then do people, a part of Nature, behave so contrary? Nature works to preserve energy. The body works in a very efficient way. People throughout the world have fashioned their highest aspirations as religion. It is reasonable given the appearance of spirituality being a part of humanity that our religious inclinations are true and atheism is just a recent trend or correction in the stock market of humanity's thinking.

If a work of art grabs someone's interest, is this art appreciation fake? We value art. Museums are not repugnant to the atheist. Schopenhauer substituted art for the mystical drive and this becomes palatable to the European Man of Enlightenment. Give us no God, but give us Art.

Art is a poor substitute.

Schopenhauer struggles with willing. He misses the point, for Schopenhauer contemplates the World, is bothered, and stays with the World being a problem.

Some people sense the divine like some people are artistic or mathematical. Some people know things in reality others do not. Some people feel insecure and must say there is no God so the rational mind stays in control. but it isn't in control.

It is natural to want to hedge your bet, as life is uncertain. It is natural to express gratitude if things turn out well. Gratitude turns into worship.

Nature is not inclined to waste energy. People are not stupid for believing in God. being not stupid means not wrong. Why would this reasonable machine called Nature act so unreasonable with its most reasonable bunch of creatures? That in itself does not make sense so we might think there is a truth to God.

Be that as it may, let me share what i have learned. Atheism is a belief. Without a possibility of really knowing, an honest answer would be to state the likelihood of God as something uncertain, yet God either exists or does not exist. It is obvious we cannot prove there is no God and no proof would prove God does exist to those not convinced. It is a stalemate, so I take it in general that God is a hypothesis and most people are fibbing in their religious statements. It is easy for an individual to confuse belief and knowledge as inductive reasoning borders on conjecture and belief.

Once society gets going we have a situation of Power, coercion, and inequality. Beliefs are part of the structure of survival in society so members may be reasonable to listen to coercion and believe unreasonable ideas without thinking about it too much.

Pythagoras is the father of philosophy. His was a mystical philosophy, but it is Plato, Socrates, and Aristotle who are thought of as being the philosophical tradition of Ancient Greece. I was genuinely surprised to read Plato's account of Socrates for in the dialogues, Socrates comes off mentally like the Peanuts character, Pig Pen, for Socrates stirs up a mess wherever he goes. His questions are left dangling as they come up with no answers. just questioning and questioning and further questioning. Socrates questions whether people know what they mean when they say certain things. They may think they know, but their lives were busy with commercial affairs, unlike Socrates who concerned himself with Higher pursuits and could spend his time asking questions without the need for answers.

Socrates finds other people's thinking to be deficient, as they could not answer questions whose design was to pummel, not derive answers. Socrates wants to prove the Oracle right, that he is smarter than others. Socrates is superior in his mind, as others cannot find answers to his questions that satisfy him. but the people had no reason to provide answers, as they were busy with productive lives. They didn't stop to question what seemed okay to them.

Socrates was put on trial because students of his wanted to take over Athens. They killed people and took what wasn't theirs. This is why Socrates was on trial. He was on trial for his life. If there was a time to provide some answers this was it, but Socrates who thought he was so smart when he asked the questions does not have it in him to answer questions directed at him. The shoe is on the other foot. Instead of giving us the courtesy of a reply, he would rather die.

In reading history and philosophy some people seem more honest or genuine to me than others, but I take it that everyone wants to know the truth, but Power corrupts. To communicate effectively the meaning of what is to be communicated must be understood by the other. It is understood within the Public or commonly understood definitions of words and concepts.

Cognitive dissonance arises. Some people, such as myself wish to describe how the world behaves. I twist words to mean what I want the words to mean with the caveat that the use of any single word and groups of words are true in their usage. I cannot just use a word to mean what I want it to mean. I have to use it in a way to show the word does mean what I want it to mean. Many people want the world to behave according to their belief , not how it behaves. This is cognitive dissonance. Problems arise when our viewpoints differ.

A group of people could have a War Lord, King, or Boss who is autocratic and it could and has worked out for the benefit of all in that community. Communism is Christianity in theory as far as share and share alike, but in practice neither has worked because people are people. Hypocrisy is Cognitive Dissonance. It keeps us from seeing we might be the problem, so we can't solve the problem. The problem is insisting something which has a problem does not have a problem. It is holding onto our private view when our private view is not as accurate as our environment warrants.

I wish to understand the twist, the turn, the shift when good things go bad. Socratic thinking is not helpful in achieving a desired result. It does not seem to produce the Good, which is its goal. It is a haphazard approach. Aristotle has a rudimentary start, but science slumbered in Europe until the Scientific Revolution, tho things were not so glum or dumb throughout as every child thinks and explores using a scientific method naturally. We come from a base of not knowing and start from there. Rules are picked up and arranged as the rest of the material obliges. We were little explorers operating on our own using the method we came equipped with, our brains and the rest of us. We learned fast and it was swell until things slowed down when we began to think as trained and we obeyed whether we did or not as there is no choice in how things go. They went and we did not have much to say of consequence as we went about our lives doing what we did until we didn't. We drop dead from exhaustion, from vermin, disease, malnutrition, and violence. From accidents, from murders, from accidental deaths to planned ones. How we've learned. We learned Europe was not the brightest spot on the map. The Chinese had gunpowder!!. (what an explosive idea that is!) Gunpowder is mentioned by Roger Bacon in 1267 (gunpowder was first heard literally in Europe in 1241 as the Mongols attacked Hungary.) along with the scientific method which he, Roger in part credits the Muslims scholars for. The scientific method as a way of exploring our universe is a natural way using the intellect. It is testing as we go with insight. It is how nature operates. We investigate the world using all our faculties. The Socratic Method which has dominated the legal mind of mankind as it is designed to produce a winner and loser about subjective qualities, appeals to some quality other than facts, is a world of words only. It is only discussing known words with known words. It's being caught in how we feel about things, here where we are stuck. The Socratic method is a means of investigating reality where you question the final or overall wisdom of things. In life we do not know the ending, so the Socratic method was never an intelligent method for humans to use. Excellent for lawyers however. The problem or the scary thing for some people is with inductive reasoning you are not proceeding with the fiction you know the final answer until you get the final answer.

Hippocrates, considered the Father of Medicine had a healthier effect as a thinker than Socrates and Hippocrates lived a hundred years before Socrates. What allowed Hippocrates to be a better thinker in medicine than the physicians of his time is he went ahead and observed in a systematic way and wrote about it. Now, my belief is most all of us go about life in a systematic way of some sort, we can use some tutoring but we all think naturally. We would think in a systematic way no matter when and where we lived. It is the prevailing customs, which aid or limit the individual in their individual lives. In essence, Hippocrates' contribution to the human races' welfare is to develop a method for investigating and basing actions based on one's reflections through the method of how to proceed. Socrates leads us into a mess of words and we've been talking about it in like manner ever since. Roger Bacon who lived and wrote in the 1200's was a fine scientist and used the scientific method to some degree, but it was his namesake Francis Bacon who formalized the scientific method in 1605 (or 1623). Galileo was doing so much science at the time, it is easy to see Francis Bacon was not responsible for creating the type of thinking science entails but he put it on the European map, and the map for the world, to have science understood in a way which works. To summarize, the Socratic method of thinking which led to the Scholastic way of thinking which dominated the academic centers of learning during the mid-ages was deductive and dogmatic. It deduces from the known back. Francis Bacon is a landmark in science for establishing inductive thinking as a basis for the scientific method of exploration through experimentation. We do not however, proceed with absolute certainty, but with a statistical idea of how things are going.

As far as the direction of science itself, there is a degree of separation at this time of Bacon between the Empiricists and the Rationalists; the difference being empiricism takes as evidence only facts observable to the senses while metaphysics is frowned upon. An intuitive grasping is not where the empiricist starts, they could not take a quantum leap for the empiricist starts by looking at the facts. Rationalists tended to metaphysics and think about what to do.

the empiricists' (logical positivists') argument is silly. They want to put rules on how to explain how we go about explaining when figuring out how we explain is what we are trying to explain. They are putting the cart before the horse. They are like the Catholic Church putting rules on how science is to be conducted. The empiricist is overlooking one bit of evidence; they do not know. It is the not knowing which allows the freedom to knock around the stuff we do know to figure out what we are trying to figure out. Also a bit of evidence is the reason why the person is doing whatever investigating they are doing. The reason for their interest gives an angle on figuring out how they are going about it. The empiricist's view of wanting to limit what's to be thought of as kosher for evidence and the

ways of going about trying to get that evidence is a limit on the freedom of those investigating. To fully state all the rules for investigating would be to assume we know the rules. It would limit our ability to improvise into a capability greater than the method we are using if we limit ourselves to what we know or how we know. For the evolutionary biologist the guiding light on the aim of the decision making process would be the evolutionary process. For we think like hens peck, ideas gambol or gamble. we proceed playfully or unconsciously betting as if we know what we are doing. But we have an idea. We've been doing this for a long time. We have to have some idea of knowing what we are doing or we wouldn't be here.

I side on the side of the rationalists. I think the mind intuitively grasps what we are doing and proceeds from there. It is in the grasping or the intellectual reach of the questioner that the answer is found; otherwise all science students should score the same grade on a test. In a controlled situation like a test on covered information, would the test scores be perfectly predictable? There are so many variables. Accidents happen, or do they? Accident is a point of view. It is semantical. Accident and predictability are twins. They make sense because of one another. An accident is a degree of unpredict-ability as predicted in the form, "I told you this would happen."

No matter how stupid you are, or i am, some-one is behaving in a way they somehow think to themselves is in their best interest. They cannot in-tentionally contradict themselves. If someone has intentionally contradicted themselves, they have ac-tually behaved as they intended, so it is no contra-diction. to contradict is to go against what is stated or true. So any intention has to be at a certain level non-contradictory and not other then stated or true, i.e., not dumb, but it might be forced into behav-ing in contradictory ways. People are forced to act contrary to their best interest. They are forced into being dumb.

Plato had to be doing something right to get his Academy to be so successful. Plato had the space for a center of learning, which it continued to be for a long time attracting some of the brightest people eager to learn. People like longevity. What is known and admired about the Roman Empire is longevity. We humans like things that last, but we also want things to be good, not just to last. What good is it if you are miserable? Rome went about conquering other people, ruining their lives. What is so good about that? It lasted and it created an Empire. It wanted to be inclusive, to work as a nation, which usually worked. It didn't with the Jews. The Romans were happy to live and let live (or die as the case may be.) They just wanted to conquer + control. To tax. To make roads to transport wine and olive oil out and goods back to Rome. The Romans were fine with the people they conquered to continue to worship the gods they already did. (after many were sold into slavery or killed.) This was in everyone's interest to have freedom of religion, but this did not work in the land of Judea. The Jews were difficult. Known as the stiff necked people they rebelled and were put down in wars which took more man power to control than Rome thought would be necessary. I mention this to say Nietzsche is wrong in how he views history and the ideas he went onto develop. The Jews did not as Nietzsche contends have a slave mentality and neither did the Christians have a turn the other cheek mentality.

The Jews are not as Nietzsche saw. Nietzsche of course has been maligned. His writings were altered by his sister and glorified by the Nazis. Nietzsche was the opposite of anti-Semitic, but he was not correct in how he sees the Jews. Historically, the Jews were not slaves in Egypt. What they were in reality are a defeated people, beaten by the Babylonians, the Romans and others. The Jews believed they were slaves in Egypt but they did not have a slave mentality. They saw the time of enslavement occurring as a result of Joseph being sold into slavery by his brothers, so we did it to ourselves. The Jews saw themselves as a liberated people blessed by God, not slaves. People whose existence is about fulfilling the commandments of their Lord, not slaves. The bible sees the Jews as complainers, which is seen in the Golden Calf story, but the Jews see themselves more in the story of David vs. Goliath.

Nietzsche is wrong about how he views Christianity as having a turn the other cheek mentality. You do not go from a few followers to ruling

Europe for the past two thousand years thinking you are beneath the other guy and he deserves anything but your contempt. You do not go about teaching the world to accept or else thinking you could ever possibly turn the other cheek doing it is what you do. I think the early Christians like the Jews were whiners. They had an entitled, loser mentality. They would rather die than take shit. They lived for martyrdom. Their faith, unlike the Jews was apocalyptic. They lived for the promised hereafter.

Growing up i had a general assumption i'd go to heaven, but thinking of the afterlife played little role in my life. My thinking on the subject was as follows; since I liked playing tennis i thought of Heaven as a never-ending match. What would be the point? Going on forever, i did not see how you could keep a balance between interesting and real. seemed less like heaven, more like hell.

To turn the other cheek happens in the words of Nietzsche and the attitudes of some Christians but taking offense is the norm for people. To protect what you want to hold onto, what you take to be true and valuable, and so, it is worth defending. The evil which Plato's Academy passed on is their false be-lief they know better than us, those of us not privi-leged to have attended the Academy. The Academy did not trust us normal people to think and decide for ourselves. No, we have not been instructed by the Academy on how to think and then know who it would be wise to vote for.

St. Augustine picks up the paternal spirit of Socrates. Augustine displays a strange intellec-tual mistake. In the spirit of paternalism Augustine decides it is permissible to return those who lost faith by force. He will force them to believe as he believes. This is absurd. It is contradictory to force someone to believe. It has to be their belief; their heartfelt emotion and intellectually a belief must be derived through our own thinking. being told what to believe is not belief. It is the improper use of force by an Authority, which has no real claim on truth.

Did Augustine see humans who lost faith as dumb farm animals who must be beaten into submis-sion? The parental authority of the Catholic Church is indefensible. The Pope has no real authority. I dare him to say otherwise. Speak the truth Pope. do you know and does it have anything to do with Jesus? did you need his love? did you need his forgiveness? You too worked in the Halls of Nazi Administration while your brothers in faith were disappeared.

Augustine had a problem with his libido, how the other boys would boast of their conquests whether real or imagined. Augustine felt he too had to tell of his sexual nature, and so the world has suffered for his sin, the sin of telling tales. but Augustine could never get past his sinful nature, and he could not let us forget it either. real or imagined.

Philosophy has changed through history, but it has stayed the same in its quest, someone wanting to know what they can know. What can we know? There are limits, but some limits are just human taboo.

Philosophy seeks to understand. Not to force one thing to be another, which is what Augustine did and the Catholic Church has done ever since with the right to do so decreed by its own say so, not because God thinks it's good to force people to say they believe something when they do not.

Judaism is a boring religion. It is a rational religion with the caveat; there are certain things we do not question. and hey, in its defense and for the defense of all bureaucrats here in the Halls of Nazi Administration, it's not possible to know or question everything. You have to take the word of certain authorities on faith. There is no reason not to in many or most instances and there is no means to test their word at times, so it is pointless to question everything all the time.

Judaism fell under the sway of one man and has been numbing minds ever since. destiny thru density of thinking. Moses Maimonides made it less Jewish in spirit and more rational, ever more thoughtful. This was the view of Rabbi Crescas, that Maimonides gave Judaism an Aristotelian twist. Judaism, a religion of revelation became one of philosophical deliberation, with the emphasis less on praising God's love then seeking knowledge. Rabbi Crescas, who lived a hundred years after Maimonides challenged the reliance and reliability of using Aristotle's logic. This in turn had an effect on Spinoza.

I like Spinoza, but he too overstates the place of reason in understanding God. The rational mind is not the way to know God, It is caught up in its own thinking. Can't see the forest for the trees.

Hume makes some mistakes but he gets so much right. The mind is the designated driver. It is the witness. While the senses sense, the mind sees, it keeps it together. Hume knew this much and this is the key, the mind works for the senses, or how he puts it, the mind is the slave of the senses, not the other way around. The way is not to force control. to try. to effort. to dominate as we see our desires as bad. Hume also states many of the problems the philosophers are trying to figure out are not real problems, just semantical and i would agree. His argument against causality and inductive reasoning on which his thinking stands falls flat. The book, "Infinitesimal" which i read this past summer before i read Hume alerted me to the fact Hume is not factual in his arguments. Still, I like him.

Philosophy has changed over time. Many questions have been answered. Many questions philosophers asked about our place in the world were answered by math, physics, and other sciences because those questions were about our place in this physical world and those answers were available to be answered. You want answers, not to ask again and again when there are no answers to be gotten, unless you like to ask the question or it pays to ask the question.

People can easily recognize there is no past, but did you know there is no future? Where is the past? Where is the future? There is no now! Now is a separation between a non-existent past and an imagined future.

Would God bother knowing the future? There is no time. What's to be known from God's point of view? not much. let things run themselves. This is how much God loves us; God loves us enough to trust us as adults, not to send his only son to save us.

There is no time. There is no space. The universe consists of angles and momentum.

If there is time, what is time? Time is sequencing. Time is the ordering of events as seen from a point of view or seen in perspective. It's the passage of objects in relation to one another; movements of objects compared at different points along their path (trajectories). Moving along a trajectory an object is predictable while viewing in that perspective. Change the perspective, predictions change.

If the universe consists not of time and space but as Julian Barbour says, angles and momentum, what is a priori? How are we equipped to encounter this world? What we have is a sense of direction. A directional grid is included in any of our viewing. We view not what is, but what was and is upcoming. Our viewing is of process, or things occurring, not a still life. a still life is still when viewed as a single slice.

A movie projected from film looks to be moving, but it is composed of a series of still lifes. What we see of course is not the total film, we see what we see and base our viewing within the framing, not from outside. We view looking through us, never the less; we are watching ourselves as we view through ourselves. You are the witness and the actor. People say God is the prime mover. What this means is life acts as a whole. It is undivided in itself. There is no truly separate thing. It is always seen as a whole. Life is one movement and this is what people mean when they say God is doing the work. but life consists of many movements. We are like a conductor or we have a conductor or metro gnome reading and organizing the symphonic score, for our thoughts are like trains running on tracks. The train cars are the notes written on a score. A score is a track of notes; a 2-dimensional directional display of notes read in sequence giving the effect of time and movement yet it is all here. Is there a here + now? It is all process, it is angles and momentum. It is the possibility of the upcoming. There is no space. It is all projection. It is angles and momentum, our tensional holding. Our pattern gives rise to the inevitable. There is momentum ---> it continues. There are angles, the tension, which is here, dictates what is here for these are the directions indicated by and for the momentum. We see where we look as where else can you look but for where you are looking? and you are looking there as it is you habit, your angled momentum. your take on things, how you see it and how you do it. It's your thing that you do but you wouldn't know it as we are like fish in the sea. Being in water our whole life we are never aware of our inherent buoyancy. We take it a fight against the elements. It's us against everything, which isn't us, for we consist of limits, which are angles within momentum.

We are the whole thing but we view ourselves as the individual unit known as you, your name. This is the seat of the soul whose foundation is paradox, the flip-flop of viewing movement, which gives a sense of engagement; the eternal, the time of no time.

Within ourselves are many thoughts that we as conductor can read. Composed of many trains of thoughts what is produced as a symphony comes out as a whole, yet ourself as the individual unit place that symphonic whole onto a train of thought into a 2-dimensional way of proceeding. We take in the whole and proceed in a linear fashion, as after all, that is the way we walk. We walk forward or backwards or sideways, so isn't it fortunate our thinking is likewise fashioned in a like manner? but it's not. We are far more aware in the prior, before we boarded the train of our individual thought process. before you got ticketed, seated, asked for proper ID and head on your way as you on this directional train of thought. You were the whole. The fall from Grace is to fall into the individual you who is so small minded you think you yourself are a separate self, an individual you that got created in time and will die at a certain point. You are always and only the Reading of Your Life. You are what you view and that goes on forever, that is until I don't know.

When is a word true? a word must show it is true. It must fit into the sentence structure. On the grid it is now. It fits in with what was before and leads to a following moment, which is funny because the following is the upcoming moment. Upcoming becomes the following. Following is usually in the past but the future follows.

The word, which was the present moment, becomes the preceding word. We view the word in space in sequence. These words are spaced out in space, not time. The word's meaning comes through its definition. Its definition is its coin of usage, the ticket for your passage on the train of thought but the word's meaning must also fit into the train of association, not just forwards and back on this one line of thought but viewed as a whole, or otherwise something doesn't sound right. Intuitively we get smacked, jacked up, and derailed.

The word's individual meaning is its face value, what we hear. We take the meaning to be its definition. Its definition makes it the coin to use but its meaning is also in its usage. We get this intuitively as it involves grasping the whole without getting stuck in details. It is intuitive, not thought but known. Intuition consists of an instant knowing of an accumulation of thoughts. The intuition, the meaning of the definition and its context becomes the coin for understanding the meaning. It is known, but it is guessed at since we take it on faith we know what the person means. Often if there is a mismatch it will make itself known. Until then however, it is not recognized. People are often surprised to discover a mismatch after we assumed our understanding of the meaning fit, i.e., no discord.

Enlightenment is a curious word. I have made the claim it pertains to me. Am i to be believed? My claim is it is the natural ever-present condition of everyone. It's not something I achieved. It is something I claim to have recognized, that this claim is true for me and it is true for you. While I feel I am trustworthy I invite your full skepticism. We will look at words, what they mean, and why I am claiming my view has much to offer.

It takes no time and no money. You know it or you don't. I have found a disadvantage in getting enlightened. It makes me far more sensitive and aware of pain, because enlightenment is about the truth. if you don't think the truth is painful i don't know what planet you are on. The truth is, this is a very painful planet.

The pain is the pain we inflict on one another. Buddhism is a dog chasing its tale of nirvana, the end of suffering. I just want to be clear. this is an examination of what is. A key factor in human existence is humans cause pain to one another. People need explanations. I find the legacy of the bible is not a slave mentality but a blame our self-mentality. It's our fault. We are the cause of our original sin, which existed before we did. It's our Nature.

Many people on the spiritual path over mentalize. They give explanations which are not needed, that might be misdirections, that are often not true. I think many things are accidental, there is no personal responsibility and we have to get beyond the blame stage to resolve the issue in any case. It's good if people take responsibility but too much worry makes us neurotic. The unfortunate thing here on planet Earth is many people feel responsible for stuff they did not cause while so many others do not take responsibility for problems they did cause.

I can see how everything is inevitable. Things cannot be different than they are which means they could not have been different or they would be, and yet, the future is not determined. Everything which is driving this point to the next point is inevitable. it only is what it is, and yet, knowing original conditions will not let you predict everything.

We are so busy with the world set up this way, where most everyone thinks fulfillment lies in obtaining something to fulfill ourselves, and at the heart of things our economic system is built on inherent dissatisfaction. We are selling something to others because as a society we have agreed that we need more. We need more economic growth. Contentment makes investors nervous. The system is not geared for intelligence. It is not geared for being kind. It is geared to sell. Money talks. Religions are the tools of society to maintain our norms, the norm of maintaining our life as it is. (It is natural and good to hold onto life.) We are not permitted to change. We are in a bind.

We are made to believe we lack something, an improvement is needed. Things could be better.

We give a lot of airtime to views, which have nothing to do with reality. Most people are stuck in a game of make believe. People can't actually believe the shit they say they do. somewhere inside they know. but this is the story we tell. We listen to some stupid shit, then need to clean it up. Someone rips someone off. The other person gets hurt, thinks or feels they have to do or not do something about it. This all takes time and energy. The crime is, so much of life is a charade, yet we keep it up. We are "shocked," we are "shocked." It's like the line from the Humphrey Bogart movie, Casablanca. The authorities have raided the bar and are shocked to find gambling. It's a stupid game we humans play.

We have become used to the usury fee of living. We are comfortable once the pay offs have been made and we are grateful for having the means provided to make our payments.

To understand life, use a game theory. People make or adapt strategies. For the basic human the mind will apply a grid for directions. This is up or down, in or out. Right or wrong. Good or Bad. When we shift from scene to scene the continuity between scenes is you. It appears to have flow because the grids from the different scenes line up in your viewing. If your sense of right or wrong is disrupted our viewing does not flow.

in general: we want a good life. to limit one's vision to what one perceives as good, to be overly goal oriented, narrow minded by tunnel vision, it prevents us from seeing the whole and getting what you want.

We have rulebooks. Obviously the bible is not the literal truth. People use it as fact instead of using it for it's spiritual teachings. People who refuse to see something so obvious hurt everyone else. I love God and like religions, but religions are cruel.

The Main Question in Philosophy perhaps is: How does our representation of the World play out?
Our world is represented. It is a self-generated view, generalized by your brain while you see. We see as humans see. Not all of us see alike, but we all see alike in that we are humans.

People have asked silly questions that have no value in advancing their understanding of life.

they play musical chairs on the titanic. We notice another person took our seat away while the iceberg looms ahead, unseen danger lurks.

We are shocked, shocked.

What I know, we get caught in the net, in the game.

Questions, which arise in the story, are attended to in the story. That takes time. Nirvana lies not in the story but in the realm of resolution.

What happens after we die? I believe the Tibetan Book of the Dead got it right, With whatever time we have we review our life and judge ourselves. this takes a split second.

Voltaire did not understand Leibniz. This, being our only world,

 is the best possible of worlds. Let us cultivate our garden!

the seat of the soul might be the TMJ where the short-term muscle memory of talking hooks up with the long-term memory of the word's meaning,

instead of the fake lip service we've been getting!

God is found in what is true and holy.

near and dear.

one and only.

    Where we see the outside world and where we see our thoughts, it's the same space.

    Why does the Bible have such power to it? Why has it drawn people in? It's a creation story like others. Similarities can be found in Zoroastrianism. So why has this bible had such a strong run? What's it got that the others haven't? Adam + Eve. It's all about us and what we identify with. It's how we see ourselves in terms of generations of people. It's a people centered view. God intervenes once in a while, but mostly it's about being a person and what is demanded by your being a person. Time is about generations of people. When we come of age is when we are held responsible for our acts. Time is about harvests. time is about the earth, sun, and moon lining up at certain points to indicate it is time to celebrate which keeps the memory and order of us being here as a people in place.

For me, it is time to drop our tribal identity. McLuhan's take on it is the rapid spin brought on by changes due to technology freaked people out. The old identities did not hold. So people re-tribalized. they got tattoos. They seek out new families as people recognize themselves to be kin. The million dollar question is; how to meet God, the source of all relations. akin to being the source. Now, one might think meeting God is good, but then again, many people think they will meet their Maker when they die and would not consider that good at this time. this is a semantical problem as well as a real problem. What is ideal in some scenario might not be in everyone's immediate benefit or beneficial at all. Individually, it is natural to fear death. Our body has a natural tendency to protect itself plus we have stuff we care about and want or need to get back to. Other people's well being are involved. We might be much happier after death, meeting God. Let's say there is a God and we will be happier after we die. That has no bearing on decisions made here. If a Higher Order exists, there is no reason to bring it in here. If it operates at a Higher Level, let it operate at a higher level. Let God worry about God. If God has got a beef with us, God can enforce God's laws. We don't need humans acting on God's behalf.

So, how to meet God? In the bible the way told is to eat the apple. Eat the apple and God shows up and asks us to tell our story. but Adam blamed Eve who blames the snake and mankind falls for the misdirection, which got us here.

If eating the apple got God to show his face and asked for an accounting, let's do it again. Would God be satisfied with such a conclusion to the story as this? this crap we call living? this hellhole of our own making.

Mankind has fallen for the misdirection of our own guilty judgment.

It is idiotic to think an original sin exists which has any bearing on our well being other than the pain we inflict on one another insisting our beliefs are true and shall be another person's belief whether they believe it or not. whether they are of age to consent or not, we do not care. We shall educate! 1984 started before Orwell thought of it and the Orwellian truth is the bible and Marxism both twist the view. To the Native Americans and the Armenians, Communism wasn't the king twister of meaning being twisted.

Eating the apple did not make us leave paradise. We talked our way out of it.

let's take a hint from our legal system; innocent until proven guilty.

no sin ----> no need for Jesus. no reason for salvation. get off your reservations. The history of the west has been a story told of the followers of Jesus with some minority reports.

Adam + Eve. We have fallen to the level of identifying with a label: sinners.   Does this describe who we are? If adam + eve apologized would God have forgiven them? If God would not, no amount of philosophizing is worth it, as we would be in an unintelligent unforgiving system. the system forgives. Man is stuck with the label.

we are stuck in the fascination of what we see and what we have been told and what we understand and we go on from here. We are sinners in the eyes of Christianity. Judaism is far more complex, for there are multiple truths, contradictory explanations may be simultaneously true. take the directions which get you to your destinations. Be aware and proceed. too much time is wasted having fallen for the misdirection.

At some point we must surrender our private view. Directions are relative to the viewer but are shared in a larger sense. Sometimes things get confusing. We need to shift our focus in the experience of living. Sometimes we need to reorient from our personal grid to the Collective or Commonly Understood idea of things to get a better idea. Everyone does this naturally. Certain things must be held onto in order to be ourself. you can only let go when you are able to and it's not always a good time to let go. Sometimes the situation is not one which may be dealt with. We know when it's time to surrender our personal point of view. Some situations are easy. Sometimes we must work to merge or understand.

the cool thing is, your inner private view is correct, but this often involves the removal of inauthentic strategies, which got you so busy you forgot who you are. Everything acts according to its nature. Will acts at moments but overall, nature is how something behaves. We may will to act, but we act according to our nature.

This universe sucks. that is yin pulling us in; the start of life as breath, as a beat, as a pulse. it concentrates. it builds and unleashes. it lashes out in the blink of an eye, a universe expanded. the yang and the yin. the near and the far. top sided and screwed tightly.

the hand is quicker than the eye but the mind can see the hand in different frames of reference. The physical must stay as the physical and move as the physical. The mind is our complete representation but the mind can jump around. and it jumps to right or wrong conclusions.

the mind is within conditions but the mind is framing the view and the mind can reframe the view. It's not the job of the mind to know itself, it's got a job to do, but it likes to learn. it likes to look around at things and it learns by looking at things. the mind is certainly aware of itself. I see no need for another self than the conscious activity of the self. this sounds like mind to me. some people might like to keep a duality going, a mind body problem. to me, it all seems one.

Is there a Self other than the mind? The Self knows itself looking thru its mind.

the goal is to unjam the works so it functions. The universe works. We've got the will and the manpower. We have an executive socio-economic model problem.

i don't sense a problem in myself. I do not sense a personal self in me or my experience. I have howard who i grew up as and is what I call myself and think of as myself. I'm Howard, but underneath I'm this thing that has the ability to be Howard. I don't think of myself as any particular self or to be me. I just happen to be me, for i am a circumstantialist who happens to be howard, who does have a personal sense of being Howard, just not all the time and not primarily. I'm what stage Howard is at. and at this stage, i happen to be Howard, who is saying,

Kant got it wrong. It is not the intuition of space we have a priori. We have an intuition not of space but a directional grid. If we don't project space, what do we display? this is a directional grid for what? for directions. and who is there a priori to use the directions? the directions themselves as seen intuitively.

the a priori intuition is the intuition. It intuits itself.

awareness is aware of itself and this is the primordial intuition. awareness is aware of itself because that's what it is, it is aware as awareness. Awareness is aware by means of its intuition; it's being aware of itself as aware. It knows what it senses by the intuition of its awareness of what it senses. what it senses are the directions.

the intuition intuits the directions of the intuition intuiting directions, which are directions of itself as it is aware.

The a priori intuition is the intuition. It intuits itself. What enters it. and how it went about it. It has an idea as things happen, enfold, get processed. the memory knows the memory by how it stored itself. and it stored itself in the way it got created, an enfoldment of action. the processing of itself being itself.

on one level this universe is all talk, no action. and then we go and describe ourself. the thing in itself would be the thing in itself and it would not be mental pictures but mental picturing. It would be a feel of itself as it reacted. It got to know through itself as it thought and felt for itself. so it would enfold the information not as pictures, but as it pictures. and this would be more in the nature of how it pictures rather than of what it pictures. It has a feel for the thing because we've gone through this before. I know where this is heading because it reminds me of the directions this thing took before, whether it is music, visual, or smell, touch, there is a pattern. It is in the patterning. We exist as less than nothing. We do not exist in space. We do not exist in time. We exist in the wondering of this.

What is this? It is patterns encoded in something which imagines time + space. that would be the thing that makes sense of its experience; the intuition or sense of ourself; which is a summary of information presented as a summary which would include actions + timing; sequencing in which the actions make sense to one's self as this is the inter- pretation of what is happening to us.

It beats. It has rhythms. We detect signals + patterning. The underlying mentalese is a Morris Code. more in the sense of touch, rather than visual. It is vibrations which may be visualized as hearing, Visualization means perceptible. The info has got to be perceptible.

Now we are experiencing according to McLu- han a time where technology has extended our nervous system, our informational processing. We have a feeling because things seem so familiar or strange. Intuitively we have no time to think. We've already thought and now we see what we thought. Mentalese, the language our mind speaks to itself is probably primarily thought I would think. a thought would be information encoded in a way which makes sense to that person, whatever its primary mode of knowing would be. that would be the sequencing of events so the timing is more fundamental than the imagery. We get it in beats, in pulsations. It is faster than the visual. It would be the gestalt of taking in information and what we did about it. It is situational. The memory is circumstantialized, not visualized. Circumstantialized in the nick of time and stored in a timeless vault, the memory. It's patterning is memory. Its patterning is its idea of itself. In the strobosphere of existence we live a harlequinned life.

and the name for our fundamental organic nature is kundalini.

Shakti Kundalini. We are the beat of life in something prior to time + space. We are the Form of Life, which manifests this total thing. Thank God it encompasses not just space but time, all of us wrapped up in we, but we can have no idea because ideas are processed there as awareness, not ideas. it is prior to anything you can think of.

We make time. Time is made in the processing of information. In ourself we are timeless, quiet. peaceful as there is nothing to know. so we don't know. As we are about to know, then we know.

You are in space to read. reading takes time. Are you in time to read? if you are ready.

You share a space with someone to hear. you stop to listen. You give them your time. You make time, but you are timeless within. you gave your time so now you have the time, otherwise you would not as you would be too busy or otherwise preoccupied. When you listen to someone your listening is the time of your life. You take in your life as you are receptive. You take in your life as you live your life. mon semblabe, mon frère, this is philosophy!

People like living. People like the activity of life. People like buying and selling and making babies. People love honesty and honestly, honesty could make this whole thing work. Buddha got this wrong in so many ways. People love life and there is nothing wrong in that. don't be depressed because being happy now means you could be depressed later. It's not wisdom to avoid being too happy or too sad. that is being too catholic. the wisdom is in knowing yourself and knowing you can't do anything about it. if this is Divine, it is predictable.

The fundamental problem is the ego who has to live with others. the ego who was taught by a poser, for we were all instructed by instructors who were taught by posers repeating what is to be taught.

Judgments come in the form of this is right, that is wrong. This is better. I am proud. I am a failure. Learning is for something. to do what is being taught. It may be for entertainment. It may be for our livelihood or both. It often involves reward and punishment. Judgments are cockeyed. They happen at a particular time and are seen from a particular point of view. The instructor has their point of view. The student has theirs. The visual and our private self are personal views. Sound is a more shared experience. It is more accessible to our ears. Watching a movie is a shared experience. We all see the same picture, but even then, the difference between the views from individual seats has more difference one to one than sound does. The view at a sports stadium of course is very different seat to seat. The entire screen would be seen from a similar perspective to all in the theatre, unlike the stadium.

People learn from the point of view taught. People invest much faith in what has been taught and they take as true. We fight about the correctness of our point of view. Some fights are about things and some fights are about points of view. Fights are about differences. egos see divisions in order to see sides. the ego fears for its safety and defends the appearance of safety. You were instructed and now can perform. the internal dialogues are voices commenting on the performance. Look at me. Look at how i am doing. At one point it was useful, it was necessary to self-reference via internal dialogue, to create a self who comments on how we are doing. Once learned approval is not necessary. Performance is expected, not something to be commented on. We are doing this for real. Our comments are real and instructive. We are speaking for a reason. We are talking to do. We compare to do. We do not compare to stay stuck in a world of comparisons, of keeping up with the Joneses.

What has been seen on the outside has been learned, has been internalized. Now it is you, not something inside of you. When someone knows, the discussion about how to do is superseded by doing it. You are the Master of your self and you have your points of view. If they are yours, then you know and you can have peace of mind.

Talk of Masters, talk of level of achievement, of this and that, that is for the ego. Some discussions are necessary. When the necessary discussion is over, then you may transcend. to transcend is to be free of your self in order to be your self.

the rule to follow is recursive, not repetitive.

judgments happen simultaneous with perception. You see a pretty flower, an ugly dress. It is not possible to not judge. how long to judge? that's up to the individual. they are welcome to be an idiot and you are welcome to kick their butt.

we mean not to dwell, not to ruminate, as if you had control over that. because as soon as you think it you are there, the ring of ringing it up by thinking. so please, be recursive, not repetitive.

what's the difference you may ask? with one you stayed in this world of confusion. with the other there are endless variations of the same. and so i will give my proof of God. Awareness is unborn, ever existing, it is the cause of itself. Awareness is the unique quality that let's us know we are here. We may question if we are actually here and we may ask that question due to the fact we are aware. Empiricists, people who insist on sticking with the facts would not be able to relate to another person their ideas, the work product of their thinking unless they were aware. Awareness is a Fact That stands on its own. It is an undeniable and necessary fact, as someone would need awareness to both state a fact and to understand the fact. People can love or hate themselves due to the fact they are aware. Some people deny the existence of consciousness or awareness or they demean it by treating it as a by-product of a physical brain. They deny the problem away without an explanation. If the workings of a physical brain produces consciousness i will use that information in my proof for the existence of God. Some may say a computer will some day replicate consciousness; therefore what consciousness is doing now is not so special, that consciousness just consists of the transfer of information with the very useful ability to calculate information using this information. however, computers did not design themselves. Neither did people. I am not saying there is a creator of consciousness, for consciousness always was and always will be a fact which is not altered by time. Awareness is Pure; it is not affected by time in any way. To transfer, to do a calculation, these are like enzymes in that they are involved but are not changed. The awareness which can state a fact is a fact is what is behind our ability to agree that something is true, it is the faculty which allows something to make sense and it allows us to be aware of ourself. since we would not be aware of ourself without awareness it has the effect of not knowing we exist if we were not aware. If God created the physical universe and there was no awareness it would be a condition of no knowledge of existence as consciousness is the factor behind the ability to do the mental calculations to say we exist, as well as it being necessary for God to be aware. There must be a ground in which what is exists, there must be a primary thing or the thing has no beginning which is saying the same thing. the primary thing has no beginning and awareness is a necessary part of existence, not because awareness was necessary to produce a physical universe, it's that if there was no awareness no one would be aware of this universe. it would be the same as if it did not exist, but that is a different issue than questioning God's existence. I am saying that God is awareness. that God who is awareness is the quality present in us all the time as that is the quality that the universe is both existing by and aware by means of. God would also be what everything is all the time, as God the primary cause could not turn itself into anything else. Therefore everything that exists is the nature of God and is God.

We ourselves would be no different than God when we are being the background of our existence, the thing that makes this possible, the thing we take for granted, the thing we never think about as you cannot think about that which causes thought on the front end, only the back end. so we think we are something different since we as awareness arrived here through a process of time. To have this discussion about the existence of God i am using a physical body that uses a brain to do the understanding. This brain uses energy to deliver the message. The physical body obeys the laws of the physical universe as described by Newton. We could say that God is the transmission and the content of the message about God. this message is made aware to the body by means of consciousness. we could say there is a mind body separation or there isn't. The fact is this subject matter of mind body separation is what it is no matter what the final verdict is. The mind-body "problem" can be seen from different points of view. I intend to rehabilitate Descartes so his analytical style works to describe what i would like to describe later. in the meantime i am using a physical body to state this proof. This body is animated by means of energy. both the muscles, brain, kidneys, liver, all the organs, all the fingers and toes, all the hair follicles, all of everything can run because of energy. the message that God is Awareness happens in this body by means of energy, energy which like awareness is not altered by time, it is symmetrical in regards to time. things are true backwards and forth as far as cosmic laws go i am told by the recognized authorities.

The laws of the universe as described by Isaac Newton and amended by Einstein and quantum physics are the laws we take to be responsible for what is here. These laws, like awareness, the awareness involved in formulating the laws are timeless; they are not affected by time. They, like energy are neither created nor are they destroyed. The laws of thermodynamics are not taken to be laws unto themselves; they exist as part and parcel of the other laws of thermodynamics. the 3 are 3 together, but there is a 4th, the fact of awareness. i see no reason for the fact of awareness to stand apart from the other laws of the universe as if there were a mind/body problem. So, the universe would be God and it would be alive, but God would not be limited to something which exists in time and is altered by time. God is beyond all time and space and no alterations may reach the knowledge of God's existence for you are that before you think about it.

to summarize, Awareness like energy is neither created nor destroyed. There is no accounting for its origin, for it is the origin of itself, timeless It is coincident with physical reality. Awareness is Divinity, otherwise known as God. also known as energy or shakti, prana, chi, kundalini. And it speaks through us.

What is meaningful? Meaning is built up through our associations. Meaning gains meaning as it preforms through time. Meaning is a judgment, which lasts through time. Ideas are fickle but over time we grow to tell, how has this thing behaved? Wisdom is knowledge gained through the experience of others; they paid the price to gain that bit of information. A culture needs information for its welfare, so a group of people will collect information. Life is difficult and resources are limited. Meaning usually refers to things, which enhance life, whether individually or collectively. Meaning has intrinsic worth. Emotional ties, which are meaningful, are not kept in the open. Instead we couch what is meaningful to us. We make it special and we make it scarce. Meaning sniffed the hypocritical aroma and ran for the hills. People are too busy for meaning, we need to survive, we need to make money. we need to kiss ass and put up with the boss and the other tyrants of existence. The Grinch who stole meaning is as Dickens points out, the mean spiritedness of us.

Fantasies are meaningful. Dreams are meaningful. optimism, don't we want to be optimistic, if not for us at least for kids? kids who haven't done anything to others to deserve what will happen to them later. Don't we wish the promise, the meaning we know this place has, that dreams are made of, don't we just wish we weren't so naive to be optimistic? but it's hard when our institutions are so full of crap. Hypocrisy reigns. meaning means to get sick, to get depressed. meaning is what is held to be meaningful, meaning not something we live day to day. it is something we hold dear, something we cherish. not something we have the opportunity to experience because money rules. Money has the say and it will tell us what is meaningful, as we must live in order to have a chance at a meaningful life.

All of this is temporary, so meaning is only what is meaningful to us because we say it is, it's meaningful enough to us that we would say it is meaningful to us. We know. It is a matter of definition and intuition. If we didn't know what was meaningful to us, it wouldn't be that meaningful. Meaning is what we hold onto.

in other words, meaning is the product of human thinking. Meaning is intrinsic. It is known because it is meaningful. but it is not the real thing. the real thing, it's meaningful. more meaningful than anything else.

for me, things on earth are so hypocritical, what is held to be meaningful is repulsive and/or nauseating.

enlightenment is a ton of do. ain't the nirvana i expected. it's better.

I dig Descartes. Descartes is my kind of thinker. you know everyone is so bothered by the mind body duality since it's true. we pretend it isn't but only a genius sees the proctologist for a headache. do you see the shrink for a tummy tuck? the mind is unique and special. While it operates along with the body we can speak of it by itself, just as we can we can speak of a spleen; we can speak of psychosomatic symptoms. We have psychological problems. still, the mind and the body are obviously one. There is no mind body problem to solve. There wasn't for Descartes either. If there were he would have continued with his meditations. In a letter he wrote he solved the mind body problem to his satisfaction, which is i believe a point often overlooked with Mr. Descartes, more than just to prove, his meditations were to bring peace to his mind. peace in the form of certainty. he had questions and he answered them to his satisfaction. We may find shortcomings. For such a fantastic thinker I am surprised at how he uses words. for instance, he separates understanding from acts of will. i just take mental operations to be mental operations and then I am done with that. i do not understand all these categories. underneath is one individual using one mind. It is all the activity of one's self. but for Descartes there was a difference. this does not matter to me. what i like is how precise he is. how clear. he sees what he sees and advances in a knowing style. he might not be clear enough to get his point across to us and he was incorrect in some of his thoughts but he was clear enough to get the point across to him.

the duality of the mind body problem and the duality as talked about in Advaita Vedanta are two different things all together. the resolution of the mind body problem is just common sense. The conclusion of Advaita Vedanta and my experience in life is not one of common sense. It is rather surprising at first, that we are all one, not separate beings. We are separate individuals. We have separate lives. and we are separate beings in the fact we have our own lives that started and will end at different times but the Being Who We All Are, there is only one of us.

you can believe it or not. my point is not to convince you we are one, my point is to point out that Cartesian duality and the duality talked about in non-dual philosophies are different issues.

thinking is a very unique aspect of ourselves. it does not make us who we are, but thinking does distinguish one person from another. it makes us uniquely who we are because we think in words. not all of thinking is done in words and words do not reach the level of gut meaning we operate on. we are known for skills but skills involve a knowing how to do what the skill is as well as the background for that skill. There is beauty and our looks are certainly part of our uniqueness. They say beauty is only skin deep, but when it comes to beauty there isn't always depth, so it matters not how deep a subject is when they are beautiful because we are talking beauty, not depth. Thinking is the means of interacting between one another. It is the medium of responsibility. Words are the content of our communication and the use of words is accompanied by some level of thought at some time in learning the language. even if we speak without thinking, thinking was involved at some point in the process of speaking.

there are activities, which involve time; they cannot be done in a jiffy. jobs need one to refer to a different location than where one is to get the information to think. we have to refer back to the way it is done. If the activity was learned, the understanding of how to do it is not limited to a physical location. The level of understanding necessary to do the jobs we do involve a larger physical area than where one's body happens to be. we maintain contact by phone. people are linked by the world wide web to use the information they need. it is not at hand. what we use at our present location involves a larger area than what we would consider our present location so thinking has changed the geography of where we as working individuals are. It is as McLuhan says, a global community, which is linked up. our nervous systems have been extended and our thinking activity ranges over the globe and beyond. our reach is not limited to this planet.

since we think in words, we know ourselves to a large degree using words. The use of words is a medium for knowing ourselves if by our self we mean who we happen to be and if the knowing involves looking at certain bits of time, thinking is involved in the process. the conclusion might not be derived solely by thought. we have a feeling involved to clinch the certainty. We come to conclusions using our whole person, but thinking is the cognitive activity, the way of processing information, along with our emotions, but emotions too are a form of thinking. Emotions do not use words as the content of the emotion, but as a way of understanding the emotion, of getting the emotion to be understood. there is a symbiosis.

thinking in words is representing our representation of the world brought about through our senses to our self in the representational form of words. Words are a shared agreed upon representation. Words do not just appear as what they mean for a moment but last, which gives us the opportunity to conjure up that matter of contemplation later. If the word is written, its meaning will last longer in the form it is in, that is, the written word is not modified as the memory might be. The memory is tricky because it is the record of itself, therefor it can take falsified information to be true in order to remain consistent. these become details, not needed to be true. a mental world can be built of facts which are not true and this mental world will inform the person how to behave in this shared physical world. the mental world is not as Descartes said, a world not of extension. in our mental world, we have been extended beyond what we thought possible.

It occurred to me while reading and i have since seen other writers have said the same thing; what Descartes is most famous for is taken somewhat out of context. Descartes' famous saying is, "Cogito ergo sum, I think, therefor I Am." and most of us have walked away with the idea this guy is saying his existence stems from the fact that he thinks, if it were not for thinking, he would not exist. This

is not what he is saying. Descartes in his hyperbolic skepticism questions whether he does exist. He
needs a method of determining if he is indeed existing. It's as if he is in a dream and he says to himself
he will be pinched and then know he is dreaming
perhaps, but he is indeed awake, as determined by
the agreed upon pinch. thinking is his pinch.

Descartes is awake in his dream as he is
thinking.

I have never been able to come to a level of
certainty in what I know. I do not share that grounding in my mind as Descartes finds he can for i see
all things vanish. all knowledge is built upon shift-
ing sands. the first premise must be stated and all
subsequent truths are based on an initial assumption. whether it is because i am a neurotic jew or i
just recognize there is no final word on the matter of
thinking. new thoughts will always be generated so
the trick to do as any Zen master knows, drop the
mind. to drop the need of relying on words for the
grounding of your self. you are based in something
not yet known. knowledge is a raft on this sea of
information. knowledge is something to get you to

where you are going, not an end in itself, unless you want to stay on a raft forever, a small bit of imprint, knowing what it does. a postage stamp on the message in a bottled up raft.

Descartes bases his certainty on his method of thinking. As it is based on a self-stated principal it is known as the Cartesian Circle. for me, any stated knowledge, no matter how certain can be doubted by one's self or another idiot, so i find my certainty to also exist in a circle, an endless circle of self questioning just what was deemed to have been stated to be true so we state it again as this is the circle of endless thinking, the club known as neurosis.

treading water with the frantic rethinking of neurosis keeps one afloat in the uncertainty of life. the only choice when one's raft is gone and the choice is to sink or swim and in this mental exercise no body exists, only a mind and it does what it can, it spins in place. /

neurosis is a club. language is the means of joining the club. language is a means of communicating the message of our membership, the rite of passage, and the eternal damnation of endlessly going over the same thing again in the midst of going over it again, and in case you did not get the message the first time, you get another opportunity to express one's self with the calling card of our inner allegiance. let us honor our commitment by repeating the lessons of what we are learning, what we are doing, and how could we do this any better?

people are stuck in a cycle of reward and punishment. most people operate on the level of behavioral conditioning. Because we fashion life as a carrot and a stick. What means have we to punish? There is the physical and the mental. surely the mind and body are the same and they are different. what is the best way of teaching? to have a teacher who knows what the hell they are talking about. and this is rare. rare and fun.

people are stuck in the cycling of apprehension, misconception, and mis-identification. there is no free will. the idea does not make any sense. how would you know? the free person is free to be how they are. the unfree person is someone whose mind wanders. the free person will say i am happy as i am.

the person who is captivated by the carrot thinks of other things. Free will is not what people want. it is the wrong subject. Give me liberty. That is the freedom people want, not free will. you are who you are, the only thing which limits free will is to not see what is here.

the free person is free to see they need more liberty. the person speaking of free will is blowing smoke out their ass. peeing in the wind. to speak of free will is to be a stooge. It is my opinion people are not enjoying the natural state of enlightenment for a few reasons. We have been taught that the state is something else. As we appear in this process of evolution we are caught in the net of time. our decision making process is limited by our thinking we are limited to what we appear as. The intuitive faculties are subtle. They did not have the means to provide as quickly as other attributes available. Brute strength has been the ruling power because face it, it can do the job quicker than some dreamy new age dreamster. but brute force will not get you to where you are going. so we are left here knocking our heads against the metaphysical wall.

if there is a freedom to choose as a form of freedom of will, this means for most people the freedom to make the wrong choice. much of the lessons to learn from life is to delay gratification and most people imagine free will as the freedom to do what they choose, but it isn't, it's the freedom to learn. and it's the freedom to learn what you want to learn, as well as understanding your freedom might be a mistake. freedom is not the solution. freedom is not the prescription for happiness which is what people want. to talk of freedom is to talk of something else, which only complicates the discussion. is there something to get free from? there are spiritual paths that work. we have different temperaments. the path itself is the goal is the solution to happiness. if you are on the right path and you have friends to share it with, life could not be more meaningful. God is the meaning of all of this. sorry, i hate religions so i am so disappointed to tell you it is about God after all. oh well. free will is having to go through this without choice to give you the opportunity to learn by doing. We learn in part by making mistakes.

the free person is free to see they are happy or they are not happy. the free person is free to see if there is a problem or if the problem is only imagined. there are real problems and then there are spiritual problems, which do not exist. God is always present and the conditions we have created are always present. who rules?

God is the freedom and liberty of us as people to be realized when we do not rule over one another. freedom must be a condition of society and this can only happen when our belief systems clear up, and if our belief system has not cleared up, to at least recognize that a person does not have the right to push their beliefs on anyone else. we can share, we can teach, but we cannot indoctrinate without understanding. No comprehension, no understanding, no freedom, no happiness. i am only free if you are free.

buddha was right in that mankind has not learned to control their appetite. we go for what looks good without remembering what we told ourselves, so we are again stuck in cycling. cycling nowhere but to the grave. overall, there is plenty of happiness, but it is so shallow, because overall, this is a crass materialistic society. people are stupid and they are pretty dumb as well. but money talks. money makes us do what we wish we hadn't done. it's worse than booze as far as the health of the planet. booze put the Indian in place so the white man could take over. booze was the force, money was the power. this is how i see the history of america. it's tribal warfare. the history of the planet is tribal warfare of some sort or other. teams, tribes, nations.

gangs to government. it's all about the organizing and the organization. the godhead is in the self organizing spirit of the manifestation as well as it's connection to itself, it being the godhead.

to continue in the spirit of whole hog analogies, it is not independence that most people want, or is the main ingredient for happiness, Independence must be sought out for if needed. Independence in order to be free to think for one's self is important, but not that important until it is. Then it is of paramount importance. but then, what are you going to do about it? independence and responsibility need to go hand in hand. If society was responsible, no one would have a legitimate reason to rebel. teenagers are going to rebel. that is a given for many, it is to be expected, so it is not a rebellion, it is action within one's nature and it is not always a problem. but the focus on the will to do what ever you want, that seems to be the mindset of many. so an analogy is to win, it is a team effort. when people's will goes into the team the team has the best chance of winning. however, winning is not what everyone wants. people who are in it for the love of the game want to win, others want to look good, and if you want a good paycheck, looking good is a better strategy as there is no team in the business of baseball, there are companies. Team spirit lives in the game, in the fan's wishes, and in being for one's self, for the game consists of teams and teams have players who are not interested in the team, only themselves. and all teams have owners who look at the bottom line at various times in various ways. all players know they can be let go. given all that, the normal key ingredient is to have a disciplined team. the team that disciplines itself out of the love of the game and the understanding of human nature and the divine good luck not to have self centered glory seeking assholes get in the way of what's good for the team insures the greatest happiness. the team is too caught up to do more than being caught up. which is a good thing to be caught up in. but, that's that. most of us are not in some kind of pennant race. god is great, but to understand your self in your life is the road to wisdom. God is great, but God can take care of itself.

that's the point. God is self-sufficient. God does not need people to teach religion. God does not care to be known or not known. God is beyond caring so we have to take care of one another. God cares in the form of us caring. it is unfortunate that it is this way because if you look for how things are as evidence for God, the overwhelming evidence is that if there is a God, God does not care, and that is what i am saying. We can care and that is usually the problem. damned if you do, damned if you don't.

Humanity is a club and language is our calling card. the prayer of my youth as taught in the public school to get us through danger, "duck and cover."

we take our selves to be whole, but we think two dimensionally as we are people who walk and talk and proceed in such a manner while we take our self to be whole.

Language is a club and we who speak it are the experts at using the club. and how we beat one another with our clubs. i find a similarity between two philosophers in their use of the club. both Maimonides and Kant are certain that we in ourselves will never ever be capable of knowing the thing in itself. i too state we cannot know, but it is not a matter of knowing, and in this way, we do indeed know. (it is a matter of knowing and forgetting, not knowing alone.) no question about it. i am as certain as Descartes ever was. i can forgive him for many things, even thinking dogs are robots, but i can never forgive him for not seeing we might be robots if our dogs are robots, for my dog and i are one. Kant is like Plato in his belief in the a priori. there are genetics involved to give a mind an innate capability, but no intuition of space. Space as seen is determined as a relationship between objects as Leibniz, who Kant was trying to correct, correctly suggested. and an object has a size to it, so it's a little hard to figure out what Kant means. by space does he only mean the distance between objects and not the size of the object which is in space? seems odd. then i read about a philosopher named Johann Fichte who wrote in such a dense very difficult to understand style, he was at first mistaken to be Kant, both of them beyond the capability of anyone else understanding what they actually mean. I like that Fichte finds fault in Kant's use of a priori, but then i go on to discover (for myself, obviously i am reading the information so it is no discovery) Fichte was a forerunner of the Nazis in his embrace of nationalism. Fichte, who started off in his philosophical career extolling freedom turns to authoritarian control when he got to run the philosophy department. He liked how at first the shoe fit on the one hand and then on the other foot the shoe worked as a boot when he was in charge. His philosophy suited him. He tailored his thinking as his circumstances changed. he sized things up his way.

does it matter what is real if we can't determine what is real? kids love teddy bears. a teddy bear's love is as real as mommy's if it brings the kid some peace and quiet. the power of the proxy.

we do not have an intuition of space. most of us are two-dimensional beings consisting of height and width but no depth. We walk and talk and look upon surfaces to see. it is only by a superimposition of one eye's image upon the other do we get depth stereoscopically. Time is known after the fact. We do not have an intuition of time before hand. We have the experience of living in time after the fact, not before, Our living makes time, and our knowledge of time is the trail taken during the period known as time or duration. the third dimension of volume is also discovered through movement. by our moving through space we get an idea of space. We do not know time before it happens. the Concept of time came after facts and we do have ways of sensing time, such as anticipation, tiredness, and reviewing activities that occurred. the container for our memories is time. it's an imagined place to think about things, also known as hell and a prerequisite for heaven knows what else. time and space are both realms, which occur to the perceiver as containers for their experiences. the idea of space is made by creating the idea of space by moving. otherwise it would be still and there would be no idea of space. the individual would be asleep. if we are awake, we are moving. the body is never still. stillness in the body only happens when it flatlines out. and that is the end of that then and there. life is only known through movement. moment by moment, movement by movement. thus we make our way in this imagined experience of living where knowledge is a best guess until further notice. that is the only certainty allowed in the realm of knowledge for the individual. certainty is what you would bet your life on. thus we stake our presence in our predicament. the future is predictable by means of the past. the present is the means of making the past's lessons into a future. change or stay the same. the same can only stay the same by changing the same into the same. otherwise the same would turn into the future. which is the same but different. before it was the same for now. now it is the same forever.

it's natural to evolve. it's unnatural to hold on after the bell. everything else is moving on, what makes us think that what needs improving is to be kept in its place? We are moving on whether we want to or not. we've got to. America is a scary place. America walks and talks and carries a big stick. America is no different than anywhere else. we are people and all people come with assholes and brains. dicks and cunts. that's us. we did it the old fashioned way, we took it and this is what we mean by earn.

i'm an american. it is my country, it is my club. i'm privileged to be a member of the country club called america, as membership has its privileges. as a nation of dicks and cunts we get to act like assholes and think God granted us the freedom to do unto others as we would do unto them. free will is another name for an undisciplined attitude. it is how we act, not our right to do so. the problem with free will is it costs too much when people act as if they know what they are talking about. our attitude is, why be a member of a club without using it? we are known by the use of who we are and we speak of that when we speak. in america we learned the right to do is achieved by doing. if america waited until it was right we would never get there. we have to admit our mistakes. the best way to achieve this would be to honor the memory of the man who wrote Helter Skelter and The Prosecution of George W. Bush For Murder by putting George W. Bush on trial for war crimes. only by our taking responsibility for our actions may we be free. Freedom is achieved by paying for it. George W. Bush needs to be held accountable for what he has done not just to our country, but ISIS is the legacy of the brain of George W. Bush. George W. Bush does not deserve to enjoy freedom for the remainder of his days. i hope by my actions i take part in Clarence Thomas's removal from the Supreme Court and for George W. to get to know the view from an 8'x10' enclosed spot to contemplate the troubles he has wrought.

George W. is to America as Charles Manson was to his followers. both cajoled their duped listeners into doing the wrong thing at the wrong time. Charlie is the stooge. George is the monster to be put in a cage.

a club consists of members. not by accident do you get to be a member but by paying your dues, which usually happen by way of accidents. so plenty of members of the club are here by accident, that is, they were not planned members of the club. so the club does have some curious means of improvising on the rules of how to join. it is not all thought out ahead of time. But we do have laws and our beliefs in how our country club is run. be that as it may, even the unplanned members are honest to god members of the club if their parents were members of the club. that gives them the status of being members even if they arrived here without any idea of where or what they are. for we are like family here in the club, that is, we look upon one another as relative versions of the truth. the truth that has not been decided in this country where we are still fighting the battle of the states. sure, the north won the war back in 1865, but the stars and bars proudly flies in the hearts of bigots and other admirers of state rights. the right to not tell it like it is, but to believe we've got the right to be ourselves in this God give and take country of ours, whether we believe the words we say or not. We do not have the time to stop and think when we have been taught. We all know how language is used here in the club. that language is a club unto itself. our motto: let's get smashed! smash them piñatas. put on a blindfold and swing. anything brown, colorful or swinging. try to hit it while you can't see it as it's a party and this is fun!

last century was taken up by philosophers who thought language had a problem. Didn't they know we have rules and rules have bi-lines or bi-laws? that language has been the lingua franca until the language was vernacular? members of the club know of where they speak as language is multi-lev-eled. with it we can sink or swim. we can elevate or put people in their place which is the same thing with a difference. lingua franca solves the dilemma those philosophers imagined as a problem. how to speak and how to understand. speaking the lan-guage is one of the privileges of membership. learn-ing a language happens on it's own it seems. to the adults it is fascinating to watch kids learn. and for the kid, welcome to the world of reward and punishment and arbitrary judgments which have nothing to do with what we are doing here in reality, for the mind, it makes up decisions in any old way.

Atomic or logical positivists who dominated philosophy within science, that would predominantly be Bertrand Russell and Ludwig Wittgenstein, ruled the 20th century with the belief we can only meaningfully say in a cognitive effort what we can state as verifiably true, we can only know what we can know. They sound like they drank the same cool-aid as Kant and Maimonides. In their arrogance their mission was to straighten language up, as if language had a problem not being clear. That is the point of intelligence; you have to be a member of the club. if you are, you know. if you don't, you don't belong here.

to make language in their ideal form would be to get rid of jokes, mainly puns. they failed. and we have suffered for being led astray by such preposterous posers.

anxiety is the natural state of creatures here in time. time makes us nervous. and language serves

to smooth out the difficulties. it supplies explanations. it supplies comfort and let's us know we are
not alone. language lets the message be carried into
the future. we are bound by our words. our words
are part of our deeds. our acts and our understanding of our acts work together. language is a dual-
purpose operator.

some people can't handle the truth as you
must know the anxiety, which is our state of existence being we can never know. what will be hasn't
happened yet unless you look into the future but
what you see there isn't here and who knows what
will happen between then and now?

and so, most people don't really want to
know. they just aren't all that interested. they've got
stuff to do, and language in its dual purpose serves
that function. When we ask, "how are you?", it is
a password for everything is okay, we don't really
want to know, i'm saying the password, "how are
you?", to let me pass, not to enquire about you as
you feel the same. underneath we have problems
and we don't want to hear that. until we do and then
that's all we want to talk about as we have to un-

wind. we have to unload all this crap we've been carrying around. and this is how language can serve dual purposes.

we only know about time through our memory. no memory, no time.

it seems to me that language does a fantastic job! language is not simply language as it speaks to one and all. Everyone will take from the words what they do and we can never really know what is going on in another person when the two of us are both illusions. or maybe we can actually know. i know what i am thinking and you know what you are thinking, therefor we know what we are thinking and the act of communication is to share these thoughts. since we are members of a club, the club of book readers, we don't know one another personally but we share certain attributes. now, this is a book, but let's suppose this was a technical manual, something that actually requires someone to know something real in the real world, not this imaginary respite, this time out. People in a profession have demonstrated a certain level of proficiency. This is the requirement for membership. the initiatory rights.

as a certain level of competence has been demonstrated we take members to be people who know
what they are talking about. There are safe guards
in place to retest members. Professions have their
unique language, their lingua franca, their dialect. It
is a language built of specific words specific to the
trade. The point of profession is to be professional.
Language serves the purpose very well.

The world is mysterious to those new here. On
an absolute level no knowledge may be held onto.
But in a practical or pragmatic sense knowledge is
what our world runs on and it is very dependable.
Mistakes are made and improvements are possible,
but as far as a reliable groundwork of information, i
would say we all take for granted things that if we
looked deep enough, it would blow our minds.

Make no doubt about it, this is a scary world.
it's not for nothing that i am a worshipper of Kali.
She is nature, and nature, it's tough out there. So
a big problem is; what is real? what is true? who
can we trust? who can we rely on? It's a real world
with real problems and real solutions. The solution
to the verification problem was written in the book,

Earth Inc. by Buckminster Fuller. What a cool name. Bucky says the quicker we go, the greater the need for specification. every level has its range, its limit of what is tolerable. the faster we go, the more exact the requirements. verification is specific to the problem. it is not universal. as far as the universal verification, you exist, do you not? and even if you don't, there is no difference, between your imagined non-existence and your actual existence, because as far as science and reality goes, mind experiments do not cut it. Descartes and Avicenna, they can think all they want. for truth don't go to thought experiments. thought experiments are there only to get the idea. Then you have to test out the idea, and have you thought of the experiment to test out your experiment? The re-verification is where to test one's skepticism.

Hey, it's a scary world out there, and we've learned, or we have to learn, who to trust. Also, how to learn?

It's so easy and complicated. Thank God as far as the world goes, whether it is real or imagined, there are people we share it with who run things. not to be too complicated, but we have to trust someone or our range of what we can do gets very limited. To totally not trust, to be in a state of total skepticism is ridiculous. It's called paranoia. at some point we have to surrender our mind, that is my belief.

As far as the world goes, our collective knowledge is so much more complete than any of us have by ourselves. the world presents certain difficulties. I totally buy into the evolutionary biology way of looking at things. I figure creatures are here in time. they need to know. how to know? other people have tested things out. cool.

do i question everything or do i accept certain premises as there is no reason not to? i find certain skeptics to be mere neurotics. When you get down to brass tacks this is a world of business. Businesses rule the world. Countries are collections of people. Companies employ them and pay off the politicians, so who runs the world? I'm a Jew and i don't see that i've been running this world these past 61 years. If the Jews have been running the world, it's news to me.

the cool thing about lingua franca is it's just business. it's just buying and selling and make no mistake about it, we are dealing and deals are done. In the business world when two new cultures with different languages build up a need to deal with one another they develop hybrid languages to do some business. the lingua franca is not invested in the history of a people. It is not a language owned by one culture. it's not about the person, it's about the business of living and how things are done to provide for the welfare of us who are trying to survive. personal history often gets in the way of your understanding.

the totally odd thing about anxiety is, it is based in time. in time we are afraid of what we can't know, but here in this moment we can know. we can pause. we can see what is here to do. we can plan. we can look back and we can look ahead. what we can't do is to be somewhere else.

the problem with knowing is it is infinite regress. to understand you have to go back, to retrace your steps but you will find definitions were based on someone's word. it all comes down to who can you trust. but we are already in this world, so most things seem to be a matter of common sense. but most people rely on their own version of sense. of what happened to them via sensation, that is, experience but as Descartes rightly pointed out, the senses are not to be trusted as far as the accuracy of the information.

therefore the solution is the surrender of the personal limited point of view into the field in which it exists.

everyone does this. we only have so much time and time will determine where our attention is.

why free will? so we feel okay about punishment. but it's not needed. we have laws and we have means of testing whether someone is capable of understanding the law. the question is not one of free will. the matter is whether we are capable of understanding what we are doing here. if we don't follow the law we get punished. if we aren't suspected and caught we are technically not identified as lawbreakers in the law as far as consequences go. this is how plenty of us look at things. hey. i'm a slacker. i do what i can. i can't always think about it or have an idea. and i'm cool with that as long as i don't fall into the zone of ~~~ anxiety~~~ cause it's anxiety that really really makes us nervous, so nervous we feel we have to do something about it. we don't have free will. we have attention, we have demands, and we have habits.

face it, we have not acted responsibly and the reason is we do not have free will, or why wouldn't we act in a responsible manner to our own selves? those of us who try.

I worked my whole life to get enlightened. now that i am here i find people too preoccupied with their own lives to need to find the truth. the truth? what the fuck? the search for the truth is an endeavor for imbeciles! free will is a chance to avoid the truth. but it's never not the truth. no matter what you do, it's your responsibility. to speak of free will is to add an unnecessary level of complexity. Look at who may use their will.

if there is no real use of the will by us in this world, free will is not the issue to deal in a philosophical sense. Clichés such as you can do it if you try hard enough, to give it your best shot, that's advice for movies, not reality. advice like that will get few people to the goal as we are not playing on a level playing field. We exist as momentum and angles.

i am me for the rest of my life. at that point i will let go. I worship Kali. she cares for me as much as for you, not at all. she means to take our life and i say, "promise?"

Spanish has the personal form of you, tu, to distinguish you from the less personal form usted. we recognize we have certain times to be ourselves, to let our hair down and hang loose and we have times of responsibility. almost all of us know the difference as almost all of us know our Self, always already.

we do not want free will. what it is that we want is to be free. to be unruled. to not be dominated by nitwits with penises.

mistakes are often made and it is usually not because of language. It's usually because we are in a hurry. We are preoccupied. Our mind is elsewhere or was missing at some critical juncture. We just didn't know, or this is entirely new and we must get acquainted. since the process of knowing involves thinking, thinking is involved in knowing to some degree and at some points in time. Therefor in order to know, thought experiments are essential. the good thing for us is plenty of thinking and experimentation has been going on. We may reap the benefits of other people's hard earned wisdom. some things, which are true for other people are true for ourselves but not others, while some truths are universal. the rule, fact, or principal applies to all in like manner.

It is not possible to be attentive to all needs which are calling for assistance. Hopefully the eyes of another may search out and see what is not obvious to us. Say I have much on my mind for an upcoming important meeting. my mind must stay focused. I do not rate appearance to be the most crucial issue so i'd be most appreciative if someone points out to me i neglected to zip up the fly, as i too am a nitwit with a penis. to have our errors pointed out to us might save us much embarrassment. we can only see in order to do what is in front of us, so alternative views can be a lifesaver.

Reality is the real testing grounds for our thought experiments. Once decided the determination of how things go is not over. Further investigation through trial and error happens once the design of the experiment is out of our hands and is tested in the real world. Aeronautical engineers could be presented with new dilemmas such as down drafts that could affect the flight of an airplane. Behavior is subject to change and who's to say how it all is until the final word on the matter? Just because unfortunate things happen does not make us wrong overall. It is not necessarily the time to turn back, but it could be a time to consider. Seeing this consideration i would agree thought experiments have their place. Thoughts are not the real thing. They are a reflection, a by-product of what we are doing here. and like us, thoughts have their place in the order of things. thoughts are balanced or best seen against the backdrop of not thinking and in this way we can know.

the most awesome thought experiment in the history of this planet as far as i am concerned result-ed in the dawning of Self Realization in the person of Bhagavan Sri Ramana Maharshi. the experiment concerns the matter of who we are. are we the body, the spirit, the mind, a real thing, or just a semanti-cal facsimile? the line of reasoning is the body is a thing, which appears in time. it is not out of time. We on the other hand live both in time and out of time. We live throughout time. Our mind has an overview. We are not limited to the view at a particular moment in time, we see not just out of our eyeballs, but we can look elsewhere and in this way we have different limits than the body occupies. Our total view con-tains the next moment. Our mind already sees and knows the information, which forms this moment; it just takes us to complete it. So we are more than what we have been up to at this moment of reality. We have the next moment in us as well, and we as we do not know that which is within us for what is within lies ahead. As this takes we to complete us, i think of this as siddha yoga; the yoga of completion, that is; self-realization.

We are always doing thought experiments of some sort. We have a basic idea how things are but we are here checking it out. It appears as tho certain people hold unquestioned assumptions, but an assumption can never be assumed without the space for it to be inserted. It's just that nothing has rocked the ironclad ship of present day certainty. So we continue on, as if this is a solid, un-rattled place. But we in Southern California, or elsewhere along the ring of fire know about earthquakes. Things are not as grounded as our luck may have us believe.

as thought experiments go, Ramana Maharshi's is unique. Most experiments we know of, which means experiments of enough merit or importance in the order of things here on this planet that it secured a place in the cultural memory rather than to be forgotten away, have been done by philosophers of science or theology. Ramana Maharshi was a sixteen-year-old kid named Venkataraman when an overwhelming fear of death hit him. A full on anxiety attack about his impending demise, the final unzipping of who he thought he was occurred, but rather than give in to the fear, the lad laid down on the floor at his uncle's house and imagined without effort as the thoughts took hold of themselves. Venkataraman imagined his body being in rigor mortis and then hauled off to be cremated. He asked himself, if the body is gone, who am I? as he already felt him to be who he really is, the Spirit, which transcends death. These words described what he knew himself to be, not what he presumed through an intellectual analysis to be the case. the rest is history. There has not been a thought experiment of such magnitude before or since. this is the ultimate experience and the final answer.

plenty of truth seekers are aware of this story and i am sure more will be so in the future. Science in its search for truth is not a monologue. There are several characters and several versions of the human approach to the truth. Science is built along a road of progress, so it is silly to hold previous players up to the standards of today. We question whether they hold true to their purpose, whether they seem to prove what they wish to prove.

the most famous thought experiment in philosophy are the Meditations of Rene Descartes, who like Ramana Maharshi, discovered a method which may be said to be in the jnani style of metaphysical contemplation. By Rene's own words, he knows God. God as Rene puts it, is the most Perfect Being and by his method in three days he achieved what many lesser seekers spend a lifetime unsuccessfully pursuing. Rene Descartes philosophically speaking is a non-dualist, not some one standing in duality. It is remarkable how similar the results of the method Rene discovered are to the ontology and epistemology of Advaita Vedanta. They take as their starting point the realization of the Self. they also say the senses are not to be trusted as to the image we see being the true nature of reality. Descartes removes his mind gently from the senses. come, we'll meditate along with Mr. D.

It's Saturday, 1-23-2016. 9:25 am. listening to Low, a symphony by Philip Glass from the music of David Bowie and Brian Eno. It's cloudy and cool outside here in east west hollywood. we'll turn to the meditations of Rene Descartes and begin. I am reading the version, which was translated by John Veitch in 1901 from the Descartes' Meditations of 1641.

Rene addresses his work to the Dean and Doctors of the Sacred Faculty of Theology of Paris. He expresses his intent, what is called these days his mission statement. His wish is to elucidate via philosophy rather than theology and convince others who he calls infidels that God exists and the soul does not perish with the body. Rene is a loyal Catholic. Faith is a gift from God. Descartes does accept via faith the teachings of the Church, but he feels others will more likely be convinced by reason as to the reality of God and the soul. The dean and others have been observed to state natural reason as sufficient to prove God's existence. Descartes astutely observes that the mind of man may more easily be influenced by vice than virtue. How then to persuade of the reality of God, without the need for fear of God, for as Descartes says without any note of irony, the infidels might not believe the theological argument as infidels might find theological reasoning to be circular. Descartes' wish is not to use circular reasoning. Sadly, he seems unaware the infidels too are believers. They do not need convincing. All would be better served in faith with a dish of doubt.

let me state my mission statement, which is to find what i will find. Descartes has been discussed for 375 years in regards to his reasoning. i will be examining his religion. that is to say, what really matters; the thing in itself, not the talking of talking about it and how we arrived at our point of talking about it.

My premise is Descartes' philosophy is isomorphic to the realization of Bhagavan Sri Ramana Maharshi, not a dualistic philosophy, for both agree; God is the one reality, more real than this. The primary knowledge is an intuitive grasp of our Beingness, Our Awareness. This is the only fact of which Descartes is certain. All subsequent knowledge is built on this unassailable fact, that We Are. tho it takes until meditation 5 to get the we from the I.

i can pretend to be neurotic and spin forever in place but i say, that's a long time. so, on the initial point of Descartes, i am in total agreement. and this is what is known as Self Realization. Rene Descartes gets enlightened on day 2, but it is not until day 3 his heart and soul are awake in the realization of God. but i am getting ahead of myself, let us return to the meditations of Rene Descartes with this one side note, maybe Einstein had the most significant thought experiment in history. hard to say. both transcend, both blow minds.

Descartes is a cool dude. He knows reason has not explained the validity of the soul. Perhaps it takes faith, but that is the catch-22, the infidels in his mind do not have faith. Human reason would think the soul perishes along with the body. Descartes himself is convinced by previous proofs of God, but it takes his rightly understanding them. As Descartes himself is known to have developed a method of resolving difficulties in science, that is, the search for truth, he will devote himself to this task. He expresses confidence in his method while stating there are degrees of comprehension. He does not think many will understand him as he says in philosophy it is believed all is doubtful. Who then would take the time to understand him? He doesn't hold his breath, he continues. It is Descartes' wish therefor that the Faculty known as the SORBONNE, being of such authority proofread his work and grant the authority by which others may take his work seriously by the Sorbonne's public testimony of support. Descartes has sent copies of his work to people for criticism. He addresses some concerns. He feels people criticize the conclusions rather than the steps to reach a conclusion. He states the importance of clearing one's mind of prejudice and detachment from commerce with the senses. His work must be taken as a whole to be rightly understood he emphasizes, not in fragments.

The 2 main criticisms then as now is his use of the word ONLY in speaking of people as thinking things, and how it follows that from his idea of something Greater than him, the idea actually is a factual truth. He points out the body may be divided while the mind, not so. then goes on to separate the function of the intellect from the function of the imagination. Descartes has spoken of people in the insane asylums speaking gibberish, so he knows the mind may be divided, yet the indivisibility of the mind is one of his main reasons for thinking the mind and body are 2 different entities. given all the above, we meditate thusly;

recognizing the errors of our way we submit our self to be examined: until now Descartes has accepted as possessed of the highest truth and certainty, that which he received through the senses. Speaking for myself, i received lessons believed to be valuable as seen through the eyes of others. Some teachings spoke to me and some didn't. I took the word of those who spoke to me in a way i related to be true. I took them to know more than i did about certain matters here in reality. and as Descartes says, we take these things to be possessed of the highest certainty and truth.

Let us begin with meditation 1; It is time to evaluate matters we hold to be true. Descartes' statements here remind me of the prayer at the beginning of the most holy of the Jewish Holidays, Yom Kippur, that God knows our ideas and oaths are often worthless, therefor we pray making oaths that we acknowledge are made by us, that is, words to be skeptical about. Descartes' writing is a pleasure to read. He writes as if he is with us here now. He thinks like we think. He asks us to dream along with him. He takes us on a guided meditation. He says it may be a dream, but the images we see are images familiar to us, they have a certain reality. In our dream we are in our bodies that we move as we do here in this waking state. We have mouths that open, hands that reach and feel. These we feel in our dream, tho we have no physical brain of ours moving that dream image, our wishes are its command. Just like we experience in our sleep. Descartes was a frequent and elaborate dreamer. Descartes does not doubt the common sense view that these truths we hold to be self evident such as 2+3=5 need not be doubted. We are not certain but not paranoid. no need to go overboard. we only see what we see. never the less, our dream veers into the twilight zone. Descartes wonders if he can imagine something more simple than the simple task of adding two plus three to get five. he considers the fact others are entirely convinced of facts that are not factual, so, we'll jump into full-blown Cartesian Dream Therapy; All Things to be Considered and Analyzed. we are trying not to goof off in our guided meditation. we're going to let it all fly. we are taking the plunge. we let go of All Beliefs. God; good, bad, who knows? it's a guided meditation with no guidance, as God might be a deceiver, and a deceiving God giving bad advice is a liar's paradox. Descartes finds himself betwixt and bewildered. He is waiting to see where this is going. from the deceiver he hears nothing. no directions are given and he ponders. nothing is here. no hair nor hide. no guidance, no body, no assumptions. the god hasn't told him anything to guide him and god might be a deceiver as well. He is not sure of his existence.

after a while, all of this is exhausting. we'll call it a day. let's give it a rest, then return.

Meditation 2; the break down. Yesterday's meditation was awesome. You've brought so much genuine Doubt to Power. D's been jolted into the higher heights of skeptical mania. You've blown his mind so he is ready to surrender his assumptions. His wish was to discover one thing that is certain and indubitable. "What is there, then, that can be esteemed true? Perhaps this only, that there is absolutely nothing certain."

Descartes knows he is deceived. He cannot trust the deceiver, his senses, or the content of his thinking if the content is derived of info from the senses or the deceiver, so what does he know? of what could he, a deceived man in the midst of deception be absolutely convinced of? "Doubtless, then, I exist, since I am deceived."

commentary: awesome.

we continue, "and, let him deceive me as he may, he can never bring it about that I am nothing, so long as I shall be conscious that I am something. So that it must, in fine, be maintained, all things being maturely and carefully considered, that this proposition I am, I exist, is necessarily true each time it is expressed by me, or conceived in my mind."

commentary: awesome. so awesome. we see the real Rene. he is not saying he is thinking. He knows. He is the type of man we love. The man who will say he is here when he is here. we are not here to play games. this is extremely serious. so many people play the Socratic game of catch me if you can. we hate people like that. we are trying to live and they are playing keep away, as if this were a game of philosophical discussions and not a matter of lives and death. What we hear from Rene are the words of a hero. He is here. He is telling the truth. He is not hiding behind his thinking. that comes later. His logic is flawless. and note, all discussions about whether we exist or not is in regards to a question as to whether we exist. It is a question, which requires speaking which required thinking at some point in time to do the act of speaking, so Descartes is 100% correct in what he says. but it is not the final word. the final word is what is heard when a question wasn't asked.

When it mattered Descartes said, "I am, I exist." I think therefor i am is a summary which was written at a different time than the discovery of his self. This is what self-realization or enlightenment is according to the view of Ramana Maharshi. He is, and he has no doubt, in the midst of only doubt, one certainty stands out, that we exist. we are, and this is important. we are not important in ourselves. We are important because we exist, and we did not create ourselves. therefore we must heed the message of the creator.

Descartes is stating his realization, he is, therefor he answers questions. not like Socrates. not like Jesus. i hate people who will not just get to a point when there is a point. but that's the point, the other 2 had no point, just the bully pulpit, when they weren't on trial.

Descartes has demonstrated something few philosophers have done and something all should feel envious of, Descartes has determined what is true. The mind can only know what it knows. can your mind pick what is true? Descartes has given the demonstration and for 375 years, there have been men, who have holes on both ends of a tubular body talking about, "I think therefor I am" which is not in the meditation where the source of what the man means is to be found.

now Descartes explores and discovers what it means to him that he exists. He wishes to examine who he thought he was. Previous to today's pronouncement he says he was a rational animal. but to say what a rational animal is would require one to discuss rational, and then discuss animal, and then discuss the corresponding relations and points of the discussion. Descartes decides to chuck the past and go with the spontaneous thoughts, which spring up of themselves. He does not wish to waste time nor get bogged down. He previously thought the soul was something rare and subtle. He had thought earlier

Pardon the interruption but a knock at the door revealed two officers of the West Hollywood Sheriffs Department coming to question me about the confrontation between my tenant's boyfriend, Lee and myself. Lee has been a pain for 20 years or so, as long as he has lived with Julie. Lee yells or cusses at people often. He has threatened my life on a few occasions when he did not get his way. He does not discuss at first. Lee uses intimidation to force his way, whether legitimate or not. I evicted him from an apartment here twenty years ago when Julie asked me to rent it to Lee. I went against my better judgment as I thought Julie would not shit where she sleeps, but Lee began not paying rent quickly. He owed me six months of rent by the time he agreed to leave. This took months to drag out, as Lee would pay for one month and not the next two. So he threatened my life. He threatened my life again after I wrote Julie a letter saying i will be forced to evict her if Lee does not pay for the garage he agreed to pay for. Julie and I both knew I was writing the letter only to get Lee to vacate the garage, but Lee threatened me never the less.

This building is getting painted. The painters started working near his window at 10:30 in the morning. Lee is often out at 8 in the morning and often i try to accommodate everyone's wishes. Lee yelled at the painters to complain about the noise. How he said it and what he said was uncalled for. I happened to be there when this happened, so i said fuck you Lee. Lee yells back and says he'll meet me outside. He comes down the stairs, shoves me in the chest, and then finds himself falling along with me, as i, knocked off my feet, grabbed hold, fell and twisted, our body weight pulling us down. Lee was on top but we flipped over. We struggled. The painters pulled us apart. Lee is 75. I am 61. Lee used to be strong.

The cops ask me why my tenants don't like me. (You mean the man who just shoved me since it's ok for him to cuss out other people but no one is allowed to cuss him out?) The cop asks me how will it look when the judge sees Lee's injuries. I don't know, i tell him, what are Lee's injuries? the cop will not tell me, so i cannot answer how it will look to a judge. from my point of view, i was assaulted and was defending myself. Hearing this the cop asks if I would like to have Lee arrested. I am thinking this might be a two for one deal and i would be arrested also so i pass. I do not trust these sheriffs after listening to their questions.

Julie, who Lee lives with has lived here for about 33 years. I have lived here for 27 years. Julie has back injuries, which are very painful and they limit her life. I thought the injuries were from the car accident when a car ran the light at Fountain and Crescent Heights. but the terrible difficulties resulted from when a chair was pulled out from under her, in some sick joke. which is how i feel, Julie inviting that man into my life, which has been so much worse than needed. i don't know Lee's injuries. i didn't get arrested. i wonder if Lee will sue me or if i should sue him. these people live here, it makes meditation much more difficult. i went to the beach yesterday to meditate and now i am ready to begin; Descartes is the anti-neurotic. he is. is there more to say? to say more would be to question what is, which is what neurosis is to some degree. A neurotic stays in the stream of thinking, never to arrive at a stated position and staying there in realization.

tomorrow i'll see a lawyer about evicting Julie and Lee.

ok, back with Descartes who does not wish to waste time following the trails of both the rational and the animal, meditates on those thoughts which spring spontaneously inspired by their own nature. We see Descartes' meditation is akin to the yogic method of discrimination, the mantra of which is, "neti, neti.",not this, not that. In this classic technique the seeker analyzes the content of contemplation and that determined to be false, that is, not one's true nature, is to be discarded in the search for what is regarded as real, or the Truth. these things were previously unexamined to Descartes. He looks at life with fresh eyes.

After due consideration, Descartes says the body is not properly of his true nature. He is not his body. As to a fuller account of his reasoning, which leads him to say he is not properly of the body, it would be as he says, tedious, and is covered in his work as well as others. we, on the other hand, are searching for what we will find. we continue, Descartes will now examine the soul! before he thought it was something rare and fine. now he stops to think and finds himself thinking, i am a thinking thing.

commentary; how disappointing. but maybe i am getting ahead of myself.

oh, let us pause for a moment and get acquainted. my name is howard, the author of this book. i wrote a book in 2014, *Onomatopoetic Massage*, which is my foray getting me here. While writing the other book i got interested in what is called *philosophy*. My brother-in-law, the rabbi, suggested i read Hume and that Hume might have some connection with Buddhism. it's been super fun to check this stuff out. it is very interesting.

When i wrote the other book, my mind seemed to start to channel. some of it is straight forward. I have a need and there are models. the intro above, the let's get acquainted, it feels to me like a ploy from that alphabetically ordered mystery series taking place at a nearby fictional California coastal city. I felt daring and perhaps crossing the line to suggest i was channeling Linda Garbett, who my brother-in-law and I both think of so highly, but i got a note from Linda thanking me for including her in the book. wow.

both books will be expressing my point of view. i've been playing games there is no i, and in a certain sense that is my experience. i have always been a very detached person. but all in all, as i hope i make clear, i can see the possibility of life being fantastic with us living it. We operate with a sense of "I". that is who we are. it's just not individual. we are one while we are separate.

the thing i like about Descartes is he is brilliant, but more than that, it's that he gets to it. so many people i read are so lost in their thoughts and their words. It's so hard to understand what some people are saying. The thing about philosophy is we all have feelings. To be alive is not limited to people who are fashioned in an intellectual way. We all have to suffer going through what we do.   i'll try to further an understanding of how i, howard see advaita vedanta, and why it is the coolest of all the religions mankind has to offer. Also i will say Judaism, Islam, and so many other religions are the same religion as Advaita Vedanta, which is the heart and soul of Hinduism. Buddhism and Christianity have both contributed wonderful stuff, but overall i find their theologies repugnant, an insult to God. zen and Tibetan Buddhism are cool. All this stuff is so easy to understand. If you can understand, you can access and create for yourself what is known to be the state of enlightenment.

Now i joked in the other book there is no enlightenment. I'm just playing around with the logic of the thing and with my frustration having gotten enlightened and knowing what it is, how stupid the spiritual path is. What a crime we inflict on ourselves by making it this way. If i can play a part in waking people up to the simple presence we all already are, awesome.

Our personal self, it is not the overall final reality of you. this should be obvious. People say, I don't feel like myself, the reference point in this is you are changeable or questionable. my belief was that i am my ego, therefor i must be gotten rid of, or significantly changed, and that was my wish in a way. i wanted to get enlightened, but also to get rid of me. because i heard about enlightenment and heard so many messages conveying the necessity of having no ego, that the ego is bad, so i would never be satisfied until i was sure i had no ego, that i was free of me.

all of this is unnecessary. the truth is the truth and it has nothing to do with you or i. we are temporary. Being of a temporary nature does not make us unreal. it's not as if this doesn't matter. It all passes and is forgotten. in that sense this reality has no reality. which is its liberation. we get tied down. when i did get the enlightenment i sought for i was surprised it comprises mostly of simple psychological premises to clear up the confusion.

For a basic model to explain, i'll use the 10 ox herding picture concept of Zen Buddhism. Also, being a resident of the county of Los Angeles my hope is, as Rodney King would hope, for us to get it and to get along.

Who is philosophy written for? lots of people love it, but the people who took over have been the professionals, which builds a certain, what's the term, it's like the philosophers are close family members in the hillbilly sense. they seem to be mutations of one another.

. the whole thing is a paradox. the zen thing. there is no enlightenment to get. and yet there is, we do have a unique unmodified nature. Our nature is pure, it is wonderful.

How do we tell what is real? who can we trust, and how can we
avoid pain? Pain and suffering are unnecessary. both are going to happen on their way out. they are going to happen, but in saying they are not neces-

sary, i am saying they are not a permanent aspect of who you are.

And philosophy is so weird because as i was saying, who is it written for?

Wittgenstein is a personal dis-favorite of mine., as it seems his mindset set the tone of my childhood, that and the Cold War, the age of duck and cover. He writes two books. the first one put him in the category of people who professed his book answered all philosophical questions only to later say, uh, never mind, I am now saying pretty much the opposite of the other book. certainly something different. so, the guy's a jerk. in life, a jerk. He makes me sick. He got accolades for being so "selfless, so Spartan, so philosophical" by going off to teach kids, except he lacked any empathy for living things. He beat the kids. He had zero patience. W. was a product of his family, which existed to define extreme. Extreme to the max. it's kind of funny. If it wasn't real you'd think it was made up, it is so far out there in its pathology.

wow, it's a few days later and i have been having major anxiety attacks. which are interesting. i went to the lawyer and noticed when i got in my car i was having trouble breathing but when the breath on the outside hooked up with the nerve current inside: up pops; <ANXIETY> and so awesome, the raw nerve of the thing. the lawyer, i feel in good hands, but it's scary, the way i figure, i am letting the vulnerability of 20 years of abuse at the hands of my tenant's boyfriend out and now i have a legal means of dealing with the situation. thank god for lawyers if you need one. for sure. reality rules and i've got no problem with reality, it's when it veers off into the land of Kafka. wow, anxiety. weird. yea, if i wasn't handing this over mentally to the lawyer, i'd have to keep it together, so having someone to help me lets me free my mind to experience what is there, and what is there is the raw nerve of the thing. there is the possibility of this not working out, but most likely it will. i'll find out and there is no masking over not knowing. it's natural for me to be nervous. (It's really the message the sheriff gave me which gives me the anxiety attack, that he wants everyone behaving. He is not interested in the truth. my tenant commits assault and battery and i am told to behave. i am not allowed to protect myself. this sets in motion the presumption my safety is at risk.) (I witness I have anxiety and I experience anxiety. I am not detached from the emotional upset this involves. To me, it is part of the package and it is very disagreeable to experience. I do have a personal sense of self and i find the lack of understanding to be the ingredient to turn Heaven into Hell.)

in regards to the time element and me being a person here in time, i can see how the mind lets itself see certain things. we know some people are crap, there is just no getting around it, so we stuff it. what else can you do? you can't change certain things, until it is time to do so.

What is true for Descartes? "I am, I exist, is necessarily true each time it is expressed by me, or conceived in my mind." So then, what is true for Mr. D. is what is expressed or conceived. and how may one express or conceive? there we may find the truth of the matter. but let's face it, we really don't care, do we? For some it may be by thinking. for me it doesn't matter, one man's thinking is another's idea of music to be heard. What is creativity? Is it to ask questions which spring spontaneously of their own nature and follow the trail, as Descartes would have us do?

Previously Descartes thought the soul powered the body, but what the soul is, he never stopped to consider. It was for him, the thing, which walked, perceived, and thought. Perhaps something rare and subtle like wind or flame or ether. hey, it's 1641, so give the guy a break for heaven's sake! He says the soul was, "spread through my grosser parts."

Walking and perception belong to the body. therefor Descartes upon reflection of his own recognition states thinking is the one thing to be inseparable from him, so to him, he is a thinking thing. To get around difficulties let us try a semantic approach. Whatever could he mean? Surely, a man such as Descartes who has done so much thinking has also done wordless pondering. He has considered questions. He has paused and made himself available for contemplation. the pause is the only gap necessary for peace of mind. the only space needed for the linkage. to take longer to meditate than a split second is making it a hobby, also a necessity in certain regards. Meditation is a state of being. a space to not think, but it is not opposed to thinking, and the realizations, which arise often arise in the form of thinking. the situation as seen from the viewpoint of Advaita Vedanta is that it is a person's thinking which is the pinch creating a you distinct from the limitless space known as Brahman. the vast thing in itself. unknowable, it knows itself in forms. form is the intermixing of its presence as the act of existence. that be us. The cognition of us as separate individuals who know is an act of thinking. We have intuitive, telepathic means, but telepathy also is thinking. But to state the fact as a fact is the act of thinking. so I think Descartes was not off by much in his meditation. However, we know we are not our thoughts or our thinking.

to release the pinch is to release the sense of a personal self. this is what is known as Self Realization. also known as breathing, Being, the ground of existence.

now Descartes explores whether he would include other attributes as himself. what i appreciate is his saying until now, the significance was unknown to him. For him, by his words, now in his life he understands a significance to his being. the mere fact of being has significance for him whereas it hadn't before.

He now is making a leap of faith in his contemplation, which i do not think is fair in a logical way, but his path remains like the classic meditation practices of Advaita Vedanta. He can detach himself from other things, but not his thinking. But he is thinking. If he met a yogi and they suggested he could extricate himself from his thinking, i don't think he would be opposed. the results are the same. we are alive, we are being, there isn't much less you can say. I said we are less than nothing. We exist in the wondering of this. but most of us fashion our wondering in thoughts. so there you have it. My complaint is he says his thinking is not dependent on anything else. he should have just stuck with the inseparability of his thinking from the distinct recognition of himself. Intuition, thinking, speaking, it's a big ball of wax. it is a bit confused. let us untangle some problems. Mr. Descartes is a bit inconsistent. whereas before perception and thinking were not the same, he is stating that wherever and whenever there is a something he experiences, there is a perception, "and this is what in me is properly called perceiving (sentire), which is nothing else than thinking."

so a bit sloppy in his thinking. He has lumped perception with thinking. what he is overlooking as a statement but he is saying it throughout the preceding paragraph is that wherever he is, he has the sense of "I". and that is it. for me, i thought i was to get rid of the "I" to realize our Self. but the "I" is the self. it's the other stuff, which is not the self. that would be anything, which isn't the self. the Self of whom Ramana Maharshi expresses is the "I" which is ever existent as you. and there isn't much we can say about it, because it is silent. it is the silent meditation, the witness. it's you and you cannot do anything about it to make it what it is. it has much more control over itself than you or i have. so let it be and kick out the jam Mother Fuckers.

Descartes states the ironic fact, we can know other things distinctly but there is nothing we can say about our self. Descartes returns to consider the big ball of wax. He makes a Vedanta type of analogy in stating a ball of wax may be turned into various shapes but the essence remains the same. All sense of himself lies in the fact he finds himself wherever he is, and he relates this essence of himself in the act of perceiving he exists, and he formulates his experience of his apprehended experience, the knowledge of himself as being mediated by cognition, or thinking. He is a thinking thing. At this point Descartes expresses the wish that his ease in finding his Self be as easily accessed in the future. Nothing could be more obvious, yet old habits of mind control the location of our focus. at this time Descartes chooses to remain in meditation to deepen the understanding and to impress this day's wisdom into the memory. thus we end meditation 2. We take our leave while Descartes proceeds further in Meditation 2 without the need to convey his thoughts in writing.

i contemplate the nature of time, space, and reality. Maya is measurement. Space is the measure of itself, while time is the measurement of a duration. Time properly speaking is not measured, it is counted. It is a numbered series being numbered. it is an abstracted trail existing in projection. Space has a reality to it. Time might be reality, but it does not exist. It is what we hang our thoughts on. It's You, the idea of you.

Meditation 3, OF GOD: THAT HE EXISTS.

"I WILL now close my eyes, I will stop my ears, I will turn away my senses from their objects." "I will consider them as empty and false, and closely examining my nature, I will endeavor to obtain by degrees a more intimate and familiar knowledge of myself."

if we didn't know better we'd think these are the words of an advanced Buddhist meditator. very awesome. and very beautiful to regard. and so we begin; according to Descartes, perceiving and imagination while inseparable from him are, he says, modes of consciousness that exist within him. Is there anything else of which he may be certain, deeper than the acknowledgment of the ever presence of his actually existing?

as we proceed, we believe it is wise to be skeptical, yet foolish to take this as our nature. we are skeptical for a reason, not as the truth of our existence. we use skepticism to arrive, if we be so lucky, at what we know, not to stay in doubt of what we know.

Descartes analyzes his thoughts. some are ideas. some refer to his actions. of which some are the actions of his thinking. He says an idea must refer to something to be considered false. otherwise, there is no question of true or false in regards to the idea. Now we come to an area in which i believe Descartes could clean up his act in regards to the will. The will or desire he states, are not wrong even if they will or desire bad things. The will is the will. Desire is desire. just because the object of the will of desire is not in line with one's integrity does not make desire bad. Yes, this is true but too subtle. It is as he said before, to judge true or false is to see how it relates, and if the desire is at odds with the whom of itself, it is at odds, something is not right. Yet, he is correct. I hate the sinner, not the sin. It's not the desire; it's the pawn listening to a desire which is in conflict with itself which is the problem.

Descartes knows he has made wrong choices in the past, his reasoning and will is not without error. Things are tricky. He knows the gigantic sun does not look as large when seen in the sky. He has two ideas of the same object which appear to be different, not the same. How he sees the sun is an adventitious idea, derived from the senses. The other idea, taken up on astronomical grounds. Now, we aren't going to satisfy everyone here. After all, at this point we are only certain that I am, that I exist. so, not to get too picky in the logic of the thing, i'll just state there is some logic in understanding certain things have a reality to them while the appearance of the reality has less reality than the reality which it is an appearance of. similar to the paradoxical dilemma I Am. it is it's own proof. and in itself, there is no dilemma, it's just if there is another, that it seems i am is a Cartesian Circle. But if it is the last thing remaining, this is where we are left. Descartes is using classic Vedanta logic to say the underlying reality has more reality to it than the image. Lots of Hindu literature may portray Maya as illusion and say this world is only an illusion, while i believe Advaita Vedanta is saying existence arises from Brahman, the ultimate reality. Therefor this reality has a reality, but while totally real, is less real than the ultimate reality, which is known as Brahman. Descartes uses the same logic in regards to God. works for me. There is an undeniable sense of reality to this. we are not going to say we are the author of this. Ramana Maharshi does take this leap. He knows apparent differences are the way the mind makes distinctions. Ramana transcended the boundaries of the ego, but essentially there is not a difference here. Ramana Maharshi always spoke of God as the true reality. it's just he knew the Self was one with God. it's the surrender of another assumption, a deepening of the knowledge of the presence, which is what Descartes is up to in this third meditation. we honor and acknowledge the source as cause.

amen.

the reality of you is due to the reality in you and in this you too are the truth of what is here as you. you are not a deception of yourself i can say safely from the comfort of my home which is compromised by deceptions. that being lee and julie, but those two cannot escape the fact that they too are the truth, it's just a matter of when we find out how the truth will play itself out.

Descartes proves his worth as a metaphysician to state, damn, i forgot what i was going to say, i rarely forget and if i do i normally know how and where to look for what i forgot but this is long forgotten. i reread and it does not make itself known. damn, it was interesting enough to want to say it. shucks, and so we go on, oh, here it is; He knows that no matter how "real" objective reality is, "objective" reality is an idea in his mind. I get no hint of sophism, just pure metaphysics, just the facts, and this is true as he states it. We cannot count on what we take as objective reality to be objective reality. Because it is we who is seeing it in our mind.

nothing comes from nothing and something comes from something. This is how Descartes sees the truth of ideas. simple and to the point.

rather than to live in the land of infinite regress we'll nip it in the bud and say there is a first cause to ideas. our representations might not be as accurate as what they represent but we know this, so it is not false. it's a Calvinistic choice, some people are doomed not to know the obvious. they choose for their own reasons to believe in ideas which have no true footing, but, since we are talking about taking an idea as true which is not true, there is no explaining the truth of this to the one deceived.

Descartes knows he is not the source of himself and thus, acknowledges God. he knows he is not alone in this world. He is and God is the ultimate reality.

He reasons if he only knows he exists and there is no God, he can not be sure there are others, as he would have to wonder if they are real or a deception. there has to be an underlying reality or this is solely an exercise in sophistry, no actuality to this. That's not the road we are taking and since we take this to have a reality it shortens some discussions. i am taking this as checking out the chain of evidence, not to create the truth. however, in the midst of this discussion, having acknowledged the finiteness of himself, Descartes has taken to referring to himself as a substance, not a thinking thing. so, out of habit, he gets a little sloppy, a little inconsistent. be that as if may, Descartes is humble and acknowledges there is a magnitude of order in the difference between what he as a finite being knows and what is to be known. As he is thinking on these things he is getting lost in the idea of God as whole and perfect while he is not, and sets up God in regards to perfectibility, but to my mind, that brings in too much comparison and we get stuck in, rather than transcend logic.

now, i am not a Descartes scholar, so forgive me if i have led you on with a mistaken notion. i thought Descartes had gotten rid of the notion of himself being a substance and reduced himself to a thinking thing. perhaps by thing he does mean substance. to recheck up on my own accuracy would be tedious. I know at one point he separated thinking from perceiving and then lumped them together, so we are not going to dot all our i's and cross all our t's. What Mr. Descartes means by all his words I can only guess. I would like to have more on which to judge the state of mind of Mr. Descartes. To me, he sounds ecstatic. He sounds like an awake man, someone participating in the joy of his existence. and now onto paragraph 31 of the third meditation. This, for me is the interesting paragraph. and i quote, " because I was in existence a short time ago, it does not follow that I must now exist, unless in this moment some cause create me anew as it were, that is conserve me. In truth, it is perfectly clear and evident to all who will attentively consider the nature of duration, requires the same power and act that would be necessary to create it, supposing it were not yet in existence; so that it is manifestly a dictate of the natural light that conservation and creation differ merely in respect of our mode of thinking (and not in reality)."

commentary; the universe consists of angles and momentum. and in the duration, it is not perfectly clear.

Supposing as he says, something is not yet in existence and needs to be created anew, how could it have a duration to consider?

Descartes will now prove for himself that God exists. His reasoning follows the something from something trail of reality. not the tightest of proofs and so it is not the takeaway we remember from the meditations. what we remember is I think therefor I am. Descartes does not feel in himself a power which would allow he, who is at this point in time, to be located later.

back to the future, I think therefor I am a moment later. let us question not just the power which could bring it about that he will exist a moment afterward, what about the power that lets him exist now?

to this he declares, "I think it proper to re-main here for some time in the contemplation of God himself--that I may ponder at leisure his marvelous attributes--and behold, admire, and adore the beau-ty of this light so unspeakably great, as far, at least, as the strength of my mind, which is to some degree dazzled by the sight, will permit."

I don't know what Descartes actually means by these words. If I take him at his word, it's amazing. so, i'm happy for him. He sounds like a jnani turned bhakti. wisdom turns into devotion. to end medita-tion 3 we hear these thrilling words, " we learn from experience that a like meditation is the source of the highest satisfaction of which we are susceptible in this life."

meditation 4. Descartes finds it easy to meditate. he meditates without difficulty. He is able to abstract his mind and place it in the "contemplation of the true God, in whom are contained all the trea-sures of science and wisdom, to the knowledge of the other things in this universe." Yet, thinking is not easy. we are bound to make mistakes and Descartes investigates the use of the will and the reasons for our making mistakes. Two elements are involved, the understanding and the will, according to Mr. D. Understanding neither affirms nor denies while a judgment makes it so. It is in the will that Descartes finds himself as close to the Deity as possible, the reason being a choice between two things could not be simpler. In all other things the Deity would be grander, would be incomparable to Descartes, but if a choice comes down to one or the other, there is no room to be anything other than what it is. the choice is the choice. it is not other than the choice. God's will is so much greater, yet when it comes to the will, we are able to do or not to do.

commentary, yes, but which? to do or not to do? is this simple? how can it be simple if his understanding neither confirms or denies? Rene and i have a semantical difference. He agrees a choice is determined by forces of which we are not aware. We act as if we are freely choosing even tho we are inclined to pick one or the other choice. We are free to pick the right choice. We are free to be ourself. Are we free enough to see our determined condition in which we pick either the right choice or the wrong choice is not my idea of freedom? the answer is yes or no. it is not my idea of freedom. a will in which conditions are determined is a supercilious thing.

commentary; we are not living in a vacuum. choices are not made by one person. Who put the choice in place to begin with? Who supplied the information to arrive at a decision whence the judgment is made? what people want if needed is guidance, which is the true function of religion. to relieve suffering, not to create the artificial condition of one person making a choice. if free will allows us to make choices of what to buy and what to sell in the marketplace, that is not my idea of an accurate definition of free. The marketplace is not a level playing field and our choices are limited and complicated by bad actors. It's a mean world in which we are not always free to defend ourselves. we live in the darkness of preventing one another from sharing the information to have the information available as to what the best choice would be. We display the will to compete. people view evolution as survival. that's not what it is. the point of this is to evolve, not to compete. Darwin's idea of survival is not to be the strongest but being the quickest to adapt, to see what is happening and to improve. The strategy is to get smart so we don't have to fight one another, not to spend our time building up a troubling arsenal. that is dumbing down. to talk of survival is to be at the lowest rung of existence.

now i know Descartes is really some kind of genius. He says if he knows the right answer picking it presents no difficulty. i tend to agree. where from does evil arise? from judgments picked before their time. judgments run wild.

Descartes seems unmoved by the fact we are blind to our own prejudices. one selection is based on previous selections. there is a chain of events reigning in our analysis. our choosing is never free unless already known. so, to talk of a free will is to speak of a supercilious thing. something which isn't as it appears. something trying yet told to already be. so it postures. if all our choosing has worked but it is presented with something outside of its previous experience, is it fair to speak of this as a free will? when one word in a sentence is determined by the preceding and following word, is this word freely determined? not in my sentence structure. i am no more free than Halley's comet is to fly across the sky.

we are free to learn. Descartes is a lover of wisdom and thanks God for being given the opportunity to exist. tho he sees a lack in himself, Descartes does not see that God is lacking or he has been cheated by his limited nature. He knows we must look at the sum of the parts to consider what is whole and as they say, the whole is more than the sum of its parts. the key is not to fool one's self. also, to strengthens one's mind. he sees the mind has the tendency to wander, and in this our attention goes astray, so comprehension becomes non existent. our thoughts vanish. our idea of who we are and what we are doing cannot be held together, so keep it together or let it go. either way works. realizations happen when the mind is attentive and when it relaxes. yet Descartes is 100% correct to state keeping the mind fixed on it's subject, is as Sri Nisargadatta points out in the modern classic of Advaitic literature I Am That, to display one is earnest in our efforts. Nisargadatta continually stresses, to be earnest is the fastest way, the recommended way.

to sum up our meditation, Descartes now knows the key for him to be wise is don't be a fool. when he isn't foolish he is wise.　thus ends meditation #4.

meditation #5; our mission statement is to not stay in doubt. is our life real? is this all worth it?

in his considerations, Descartes reminds me of Dorothy who swept up by a vortex into Oz, which has techno-color brilliance, unlike Kansas, now returns and finds what is here to be real, and how could she doubt it? She had forgotten about Kansas while away. and while Descartes returns to the earth, he too finds what we take to be reality, to exist as we take it. oh, a side note. i'd like to say if Descartes simply stuck with I think, that would be a superior or more accurate statement than to turn himself into a thinking thing. By sticking with thinking he could bridge the gap to Bucky's book, " I seem to be a

verb" as we are about action and we are ever changing as we grow onwards.

i think this line is great, " existence can no
more be separated from the essence of God, than
the idea of a mountain from that of a valley." yang
and yin. the wave. yet he says, just because we
think it must be so, since it makes so much logical
sense, it does not necessarily follow that it is so.
our thoughts impose no necessity on what is. but in
this case he points out the fallacy of the objection.
a mountain and a valley define one another and God
and existence go together as Descartes will now re-
state the case. the necessity of God lies not in it being necessary by order of his thinking it logical, but
as he puts it, "the necessity which lies in the thing
itself" I buy his argument. He's proved it to him, and
he's proved it to me. It's clear he has not proved it
to others. again, he sounds like Dorothy telling her
strange tale of being swept up by the tornado, the
others are comforting her, not necessarily believing
her. for Descartes as for Dorothy, what they experi-
enced and what they now know is part of their fab-
ric. It's who they are. Descartes closes meditation

#5 with this these thoughts, "before I knew him, I could have no perfect knowledge of any other thing. And now that I know him, I possess the means of acquiring a perfect knowledge respecting innumerable matters."

commentary; This sounds like a religious conversion. As to the validity in his statements, we take things step by step. Descartes took steps, which opened the door leading to so many benefits which we enjoy today. as Descartes returns to earth he finds that you and i have a reality to us as well as the God he now knows so well. His recollection is not as vivid, yet that does not diminish the truth of what is. Now Descartes sounds like a religious convert who, having had the experience can now think back on what it was and conceive of himself as a thinking thing and remember the truth learned during meditation #4. Having the experience of God does not mean the experience must be kept so vivid. that is a matter of time and strength of mind. we could toss in grace to satisfy the nagging voices. Descartes has returned to the earth with a newfound strength for he has acquired a means of acquiring; His mind is his device, vehicle, or toy and life presents so many opportunities to explore and discover. We are the experience of ourself. Ouroboros.

meditation #6; do material things exist? Descartes knows with certainty that mathematics exists, by the fact he knows mathematics so clear and distinctly. There is nothing to say math does not exist in the world in which Descartes finds himself. He sees no contradiction, nothing to lead him to believe otherwise. Descartes tells us he has the habit of imagining what he is thinking about. Imagining is a power his mind uses to understand, to piece together what is thought about in order to visualize or otherwise understand. When understood, Descartes is able to recall or picture something such as a triangle without using the power of imagination. To use the power of imagination vs. non imaginative thinking is seen in this regard by Descartes, "this special exertion of mind clearly shows the difference between imagination and pure intellection (imaginatio et intellectio pura)."

I imagine takes work; therefor i find imagination to be the real thinking. Imagination is the prep workup for analysis. Imagination, Descartes tells us, takes a special exertion, unlike thoughts that think for themselves. that is the pure land. the mind of God which spews the logic of numerals as a digital numerator wood a tree in the Garden of Eden.

Descartes thinks imagination is beneath the ability to conceive. He thinks his mind would be an identical mind by the power of conception alone, without the use of imagination. Conception seems to mean to Mr. Descartes to consider abstract principals. Imagination for Descartes is to use the mind in conjunction with the body. Descartes's thinking is far out. He reasons he only knows his body by the use of his imagination. His body is not known directly, it is only a probability. Only by the use of his imagination may he infer his body. For Descartes, to use the imagination is to use the senses.

Descartes does not think like us. It sounded like he thinks like us, but this is not how we think, that we imagine the body and know the mind. There is hope. He admits he can perceive colors, sounds,

and tastes better by sensing them than by his intellectual conception, but he says, tho he might know
them better, he knows them with less distinction.
Previously, Descartes mentioned that contradiction
discredits the truth-value of a statement. It seems
as tho he has contradicted himself out of the ballpark. How does he know something better while it is
less distinct? And, there is the whole aspect that we
are not born in a vacuum. my hunch is Descartes ex-
hibits the illness spread by the contagion of Forms;
Platonic Idolatry. that there is an externally located field of pure knowledge. Out there, something
out there, distinct from us. Descartes overlooks the
fact that any idea to be discussed with other human
beings has already been discussed by human beings to some degree. He is not introducing a new
topic. He is continuing on with previous conversations and all conversations have in common sense
perceptions. Plato and Descartes may think they
are only conceiving pure thought, that is, thoughts,
which have not been ruined, polluted, made dirty,
disgraced, dirtied by being here. Punch line, i might
believe in the soul, which is ever lasting while our

body does not. We live on and on and on and on. We do not die. The idea of death does not make sense if there is no time. it does not exist. Death happens to something,which lives in time and is controlled by events. Death is for the Doers, not the done, it is for the one responsible, and is seen by us here. Time is where things are known. You, who are eternal. You know. You do not bother to know. When you look out into the world, what you see you know and you know as you know.

It is as Descartes says, the imagination differs from the pure abstracted intellect in that it turns in on itself to contemplate itself. this is the job of the kundalini. kundalini is nature's imagination. God is spaced out and bodiless. Kundalini is the shakti, the energy of divinity in action. The energy of the Self turned in on itself to know itself. Ouroboros is not eating its tail. Ouroboros is eternity. it is what is going on forever, spiraling up and spiraling around and around. down the hatch. the hatchery of shit. it eats itself and thrives. even tho the typical picture is kundalini as ouroboros as a snake with its tail in its mouth, that is a snap shot of a kid kundalini taking a nap. the real thing is more gross. it's the mind of man. it's the possibility of Trump being president. It is the madness of actuality, that people are actually voting for him. shakti kundalini in this time of Kali. Kali MotherFucker. i don't think i think like you. i speak in Captivity from the sing-sing of my soul.

If we want to follow Descartes' reasoning we look in the direction he is heading with his thinking. from where does he think? He thinks as he thinks and he is thinking from his thoughts. If you follow what his reasoning is, his detailed sequencing seems highly accurate. To ascertain what someone is thinking, think of thinking as a reflexive action. it proposes an idea as seen. that's the way things play out. but it's like a deck of cards in that the cards could be seen as falling away or towards oneself. We are on one side
of the falling cards to read them. we read the card's face. We're in the game and we have no choice. we're at the table and the cards are dealt. You can cheat if you get away with it. How to know what to

play? To sit at the table and play this game requires us to obey house rules. You can cheat, if you get away with it. How to know the cards, which may be played against you when you see only what you face? Here where we sit, we only see one side of the card in play.

Descartes has a certain remove in his analysis. It's as if he is on opiates, but he is so awake. he is anesthetized in his observations, in relation to his body. He is talking as if his observations of his body were of something else than him, which is how it is on opiates, the pain might be there, but who cares? we don't feel it. and if we do, we feel it as a sensation we can ignore. that's what it is to be anesthetized. We've gotten used to it. we don't have to have all the details exist so strictly, it goes on hazy and fuzzy. we have an idea of the thing. Descartes is not on opiates. Descartes discovered a technique, which enabled him to depart from the world of the senses. Descartes is an original analytical yogi. He has a clear mind. He sees things clearly and distinctly. tho he cannot see certain things. For instance, now in the sixth paragraph he writes in talking about his body, "for in truth, I could never be separated from it (his personal body) as from other bodies." He admits he cannot in truth be separated from his body. But non-separability is the reason he gave for his belief his existence to be thinking, that he cannot be separated from his thinking. He admits that sensations give him food for thought before he thinks about it, they are there whether he asked for them or not. since they are here, he sees as someone who invents analytical geometry sees. He sees things in perspective. He sees by his Cartesians Co-ordinates.

ah, he answers what i wondered about, "I conclude that my essence consists only in my being a thinking thing [or a substance whose whole essence or nature is merely thinking]." Now he puts forth the idea he can separate himself as a thinking thing from his body. We'll look at the thought experiment of Avicenna in a bit. They follow the same precept. and we'll look at Hilary Putnam's brain in a vat. Descartes says he can imagine a him without an ability to perceive or imagine but he can't imagine his perceptions or his imagination without

Descartes being an ingredient. and it's true, someone could be in a coma but awake. and we must
remember that for Descartes to imagine is to see
through the senses. Given his definitions i see how
Descartes could separate himself, the experience of
him being him, to be distinct from his ability to imagine or perceive. but here i must say, in my mind there
is no such thing as a non-physical or non-material
level of reality. when i think about existence on any
level, from the most subtle to being busy, no matter
how many dimensions an object or a field of experience may contain or consist of, it is all physical.
Given that, the realization of the sense of "I" is most
easily sensed upon waking, when the mind has no
other thoughts. you are what you are, and that is
who you are. And there is your life. is it attached,
detached? those are thoughts to be thought of later.
for Ramana Marharshi, the "I" is to be found upon
waking. It is a sense of "I" without the baggage of
memory. there is the sense of you, this sense of I is
you, but there is no need to bring in time or explanations. What Descartes cannot do, which I think he
is doing is to have a sense of himself divorced from

the memory of himself. He has been formed through his associations here, here where he knows.

here Descartes states a more accurate picture of things, " I am not only lodged in my body as a pilot in a vessel, but that I am besides so intimately conjoined, and as it were intermixed with it, that my mind and body compose a certain unity. " yes, well put Rene. and here he defines truth, "that what is done cannot be undone." the cards fall as they may. the card is read as dealt. we can take our time reading, rearranging and rereading the cards and this is known as a way of modeling modes of thinking. Descartes wants to point out that it takes a mind to understand, to take the time to listen, to pay attention. The good stuff isn't always known right away, there is much to be said for craftsmanship. a star may appear no larger than a ring on a person's finger but we know by thinking there is a difference other than noted in an offhand manner. thinking can provide depth but is prone to error. Descartes is less accurate in his musings about his mind. Here again he states his belief the body is separable while the mind is not.

Descartes has mistaken his mind for a hat. If he read Dr. Oliver Sacks r.i.p.'s writing and was more familiar with neurology i don't think he would be so naive in what he writes and thinks. His concepts would be different had he been born in a different time. It seems to me he is making mistakes in logic due to when he lived which includes how he uses words. His use of words determines his concepts. so, it's all a little cockeyed. It seems to us he is using his body to think, therefor it is not fair for him to assume he can separate

his sense of his thinking from his body. what he is driving at i think, is the fact there is a unity in the truth or the experience of himself. he is not divided in himself.

We are coming to a close to this, the 6th and final of Descartes' meditations. how did Rene do? Let us judge him based on his mission statement as put forth in meditation #5; to not stay in doubt. to not be neurotic or fall prey to conspiracy theories for an easy explanation. Descartes, being a brave man said, let's chuck it, goddam it. Let us toss concern to the wind and say fuck it; I am so skeptical, I shall call it hyperbolic. Rene Descartes might have been a stranger man then we might suppose for he writes, "And I ought to reject all the doubts of those bygone days, as hyperbolic and ridiculous, especially the general uncertainty respecting sleep, which I could not distinguish from the waking state: for I now find a marked difference between the two states."

So, mission accomplished. Rene Descartes can live a productive life not saddled by unnecessary and unfounded doubt. We've discovered the possibility Descartes had a religious experience and he had trouble distinguishing being awake from dreaming, so we know this guy had good reason to be skeptical. I'd like at this time to thank Mr. Rene Descartes for his contribution to humanity. Thank you Rene!!!

Let's take a look at Hilary Putnam's brain in a vat. Hilary is a philosopher i've enjoyed watching and listening to. His voice has a good vocal quality. He has a very relaxed posture and attitude. He looks very comfortable in his skin. Putnam puts up to shut up the nagging voices questioning the accuracy and reliability of his scientific and philosophical foundations. He makes the ultimate sacrifice in his philosophical quest to "know thyself", Hilary gets out of his comfort zone. He brushes aside all concepts, all norms and notions, all previous ideas to find himself now to be just a brain in a vat. Skinny-dipping without a suit on he sits in a vat and asks himself, "now that i am in a vat, out of my zone, out of my comfortable skin, am i likewise out of my mind? I ask myself, am i actually myself if i am living a simulation of myself?"

He has taken accuracy to the max. He has entered the hyperbolic floatation tank of skepticism. He floats there like a lotus blossom on a lily pad of wires hooked up to a supercomputer giving his brain real life simulations of Hilary Putnam's sensory input. This input is so life-like, so real. It's holographic. the tank's got an awesome sound system, so Hilary is rocking like a baby in a cradle. it's a swell spot to contemplate the meaning of meaning and how this relates to Rene Descartes' thought experiment involving the evil demon to test out our skepticism concerning the reliability or validity of any of our assumptions since our sensory input might be from a deceiver.

Hilary asks himself, "am I myself when my sensory input is from a questionable source? The source is derived from myself. I find myself to be just a brain in a vat. no longer am I living in a real world. It only appears to be a real world in which i contemplate how meaningful, how reliable are my beliefs and my assumptions concerning a real world and how real that world is. Because what I am watching in my experience of being Hilary Putnam's brain in a vat are my memories of me being me. So am I myself, if I am living my memories of myself? Would this be me who I am, if who I think I am is myself, when what I think is myself is what I am as I am living my experience of me being me, thought to be me through a recreation of the sense of being Hilary, when this sense of being Hilary is sourced through a supercomputer which has the memories of Hilary Putnam, giving me the sensation of being Hilary Putnam?"

Rene said in essence, i'm a skeptic, a hyperbolic skeptic. I cannot trust the input or my thought process. I can't even think that I think in my hyperbolic skepticism, so I do not even bother to think if what I think is what I think, for I would think, is that me who is wondering as he is thinking if I am I, if who I am thinking of myself as myself as I think as myself would be thinking these thoughts? I would think not! and yet I think, therefor I am. I am, I exist and what I do when I am is think as I think, for I am Rene Descartes, at your service.

there is no free will. in a situation there are two possibilities. the situation is either determined or it is random. If it is determined, it is not free, because it is determined. or it is random, meaning it happens in an unplanned or accidental manner, in other words, nobody is picking or choosing this choice. it is not free, it is random.

a person may choose no because of a past experience. so, a person can say no to one choice and by the process of elimination pick the new choice. the new choice is picked by default.

let us shed our skin. let us shed our expectations. We seek to discover our soul. we remove all outer garments, our clothes, skin, and memories. Our arms, legs. penises and vaginas. shedding our expectations we float. We suspend our beliefs and ask ourselves, "Can we believe our eyes, if we had them? Can we believe our luck, if you consider finding yourself floating without the aid of arms, legs, clothes, skin, memories, penises, or vaginas to be luck?

Let us suspend our skepticism, expectations, beliefs, and judgments for this is the guided meditation of floatation. In an undisclosed location, a soul examines its existence. All is unknown to this soul who may or may not know of its own existence, as we float yet another idea to consider, this, the thought experiment of Avicenna. not my favorite. it reminds me more of Hilary than Rene, for both involve a different location to begin than the one always already present. It's more of an artificial condition in which Avicenna is guiding our conclusions, rather than it being of an experimental nature. It reminds me of Ramana Maharshi's awakening, except Ramana asked himself, who am i now that i have passed away? All my notions, all of my ideas, any conclusions i could draw on my own have vanished, for I have transcended anything which is taken for granted in the minds of humanity in general. I am the Spirit which outlives death.

Avicenna is driving to the same conclusion, except he didn't get there. In all fairness, this floating man idea, which is credited to him, was not a meditation technique or even an experiment. It is called an experiment but the purpose of this exercise was to give his students an explanation for the soul. It may have an intuitive basis, but as it doesn't seem to prove its case it comes off as a matter of belief or dogma. At this time let us acknowledge the genius, which is Avicenna's true legacy, writing a medical textbook, which was widely used in Europe for eight hundred years, among others. His ability to catalogue information so the information was more easily understood as a whole makes him one of the true pioneers of science and the scientific method on planet Earth, and for this Avicenna deserves much praise. Not only that, he advanced the understanding of momentum. Which is worth noting since we consist of nothing if not angles and momentum.

We shall now consider the sleeping man thought experiment. this is a slacker experiment. no props required. no expense spared or spent in this realization. to wit, a person falls asleep and wakes up refreshed. asked how was their sleep, they say fantastic. and why was it fantastic? because i did not remember a thing. I was out like a light. did i know myself? no, and that's why it is so peaceful.

We shall now consider another experiment of the floating variety. This too maybe done at home, but unlike the peaceful sleep experiment, this one will cost a bit more in money, emotional involvement, and hours of lost sleep, for this is the baby floating in the mom's womb thought experiment. We ask, is this baby aware of itself as a soul while floating in mommy?

Babies come out of the womb recognizing names they have heard while in the womb. Babies can taste flavors of food mom has been eating. so, the baby is getting to know itself. it's not existing separate from the world. could this baby have any idea of itself apart from its perceptions? i don't see why it would. the soul is what we are, not what we have. does it take knowing our soul to know our soul? i don't think so. thinking and having an idea has little to do with the experience of being our self. we just are ourself. i'm me, and i would not say i am a soul. to say anything at all is to pollute this. there is not a word to say which could say what it is. it's everything. <---this is using more than one word to say what it is. It is everything. Totality says it. I find no need in it to call itself a soul or anything. it does not tell me its name. It can stop the mind from thinking. Why think? What is there to think about?

The thought experiment from the end of Mark Twain's The Mysterious Stranger; You are just a thought. What do you think?

The Snake Charmer experiment; drop your thoughts. drop your burdens. drop all your weight and with it any attempt to sit up. just look around and breath. your eyes do the looking. your attention draws your thoughts as it gathers your awareness, for you are the kundalini. that which exists. that which powers. thinking is hell. it is the address of your crib. thinking got you in, and best beware, thinking will get you out. is there anything, which needs to be said?

this is the manifesto of spiritual communism. You as a separate soul may give it up now if that's your wish. if you wish to merge with all that is, and to realize the Truth of existence, it is perfectly permissible to do so. it's what we already are, so let's be ourselves today.

This is Totality and we are going to befriend it. We'll understand it in the cosmic sense using the ten ox herding pictures as a means of explaining what is going on here.

The universe is the measure of itself. Consciousness is the activity or product of this universe.

Truth is the universal message and then there is the version of the individual, the story we tell ourselves which might be right or wrong. I read part of Julian Jaynes", "The Origin of Consciousness In The Breakdown of the Bicameral Mind" last night. I last read it around 1985. It seems to have had an influence on my thinking. I found myself fascinated with the premise. What struck me while reading is how similar my thinking seems to be to Mr. Jaynes. While reading my mind felt specifically attentive, a feeling of excitement, of happiness in discovering something which seems so true to me and so specific, so to the point. this is the same feeling I felt when i was with my spiritual teacher Leslie Temple Thurston and the feeling I had immediately upon seeing a video of the spiritual teacher Robert Wolfe.

Julian Jaynes shares a remarkable similarity to Marshall McLuhan in certain respects. Both men it seems have been forgotten by and large by academic circles. Having gotten more familiar with what those circles take as important, it is my feeling that they have missed two of the most innovative and out of the box thinkers. These thinkers deserve to be remembered and studied.

Jaynes' premise is that our individual awareness, our self-consciousness, is a relatively new feature of being aware. Previous to this time our species operated with more of a herd or group mentality. A God who made decisions for the group spoke to the group through the right hemisphere. People would go about their day doing what it was they were doing. If decisions were needed, if someone came to a fork in the road and was unsure which direction to take, the god sensed a decision was needed and made the choice for that person. When things got more complex the guidance offered by the Group God did not have the insight necessary for new factors facing humanity. Destiny thru density; the heaviness of the thing in itself. The success of agriculture bringing more food to the table weighted a population to the tipping point. Material gain has its price. Increased pressures of modern life in 1200 BC Mesopotamia caused the breakdown to the bicameral mind, that is the mind that consists of two houses or chambers. The God spoke through the right side, and was

heard on the left. This breakdown was "due to cha-
otic social disorganizations, to overpopulations, and
probably to the success of writing in replacing the
auditory mode of command."

This is McLuhan's view as well. McLuhan
wrote in the 1960's. Julian Jaynes published his
book in 1976. Jaynes knows of Alfred North Whitehead who wrote Principia Mathematica along with
Bertrand Russell from 1910 to 1913. Whitehead is
a major influence on McLuhan. maybe Whitehead
came to a fork in the road as his influence on McLuhan is perceptive and artistic in nature while Whitehead's work with Russell as logically reductionistic,
is anything but. It took the wrong course, as a matter
of fork. I cannot tell you how surprised and happy I
was last night to read Julian Jaynes dismissing the
efforts of Bertrand Russell as the logical road not to
take. Ludwig Wittgenstein is Russell's protégé; so
the argument I put forth earlier about Wittgenstein is
an echo of Jaynes' appraisal. which makes me really
glad, for i am a slacker guessing.

it seems the god within me explained there is no out or in if you are the narrator of the story.

the age old activity of philosophy is to know thyself. How our representation plays out are the ins and outs of the thing in itself. and who are we? Jaynes says who we are is told in the narrative we tell ourselves.

God is the Voice of Authority. #1, this is what God is and what God does. Need a creation? Go see God. Who maintains and keeps this running? God's the Absolute Thing in itself. that's the general idea.

the jnani, that be we, we stand outside of time and space and discuss these things, so how real is this? How real could i who is telling this story be? does not matter to me whether i am real or not, i can't tell. it's real to me. i've seen it's real and i go on from there. this myself, i take to be not really real. it's only real to me as the truth of this narrative.

welcome to the self-reflection, the inner musings of howard. 2/10/2016 11:02am.

Who we are Jaynes says is who we tell ourselves we are.

hold on a minute. that's not exactly what he said. hi there, it's 2/12/2016 1:30 PM. personally, my lawyer's plan is not to evict Julie, but to boot Lee. Yesterday we got a restraining order, which was only partially granted. Lee gets to stay here for now. We have a date in court, 3/2/2016. so there you have it.

I reread Julian Jaynes's book. I recommend it. He is a very good writer. Here's his description of time as space. oh my, i should include more, so hopefully Houghton Mifflin will grant permission for these words of Julian's from the afterword he wrote in 1990 which I'll include here as he tells it so well;

---> 1. Consciousness is based on language. Such a statement is of course contradictory to the usual and I think superficial views of consciousness that are embedded both in popular belief and in language. But there can be no progress in the science of consciousness until careful distinctions have been made between what is introspectable and all the hosts of other neural abilities we have come to call cognition. Consciousness is not the same as cognition and should be sharply distinguished from it.

The most common error, which I did not emphasize sufficiently, is to confuse consciousness with perception. Recently, at a meeting of the Society for Philosophy and Psychology, a well-known and prestigious philosopher stood up to object vociferously on this point. Looking at me directly, he exclaimed, "I am perceiving you at this moment. Are you trying to say that I am not conscious of you at this moment?" A collective cognitive imperative in him was proclaiming in the affirmative. But actually he was being conscious of the rhetorical argument he was making. He could have been better conscious of me if he had turned away from me or had closed his eyes.

This type of confusion was at least encouraged back in 1921 by Bertrand Russell: "We are conscious of anything that we perceive." And as his logical atomism became fashionable in philosophy, it became difficult to see it any other way. And in a

later book Russell uses as an example of consciousness "I see a table." But Descartes, who gave us the
modern idea of consciousness, would never have
agreed. Nor would a radical behaviorist like Watson,
who in denying consciousness existed certainly did
not mean sense perception.

Just as in the case I mentioned above, I suggest Russell was not being conscious of the table,
but of the argument he was writing about. In my own
notation, I would diagram the situation as Russell
thought his consciousness was the second term,
but in reality it was the entire expression. He should
have found a more ethologically valid example that
was really true of his consciousness, that had really
happened, such as, "I think I will rewrite the Principia
now that Whitehead's dead" or "How can I afford the
alimony for another Lady Russell?" He would then
have come to other conclusions. Such examples are
consciousness in action. "I see a table" is not.

Perception is sensing a stimulus and re-
sponding appropriately. And this can happen on a
non-conscious level, as I have tried to describe in
driving a car. Another way to look at the problem is

to remember the behavior of white blood cells, which certainly perceive bacteria and respond appropriately by devouring them. To equate consciousness with perception is thus tantamount to saying that we have six thousand conscious entities per cubic millimeter of blood whirling around in our circulatory system - which I think is a reductio ad absurdum.

Consciousness is not all language, but it is generated by it and accessed by it. And when we begin to untease the fine reticulation of how language generates consciousness we are on a very difficult level of theorizing. The primordial mechanisms by which this happens in history I have outlined briefly and then in II:5 tried to show how this worked out in the development of consciousness in Greece. Consciousness then becomes embedded in language and so is learned easily by children. The general rule is: there is no operation in consciousness that did not occur in behavior first.

To briefly review, if we refer to the circle triangle problem on page 40, in solving this struction we say, "I 'see' it's a triangle," though of course we are not actually seeing anything. In the struction of finding how to express this solving of the problem, the metaphor of actual seeing pops into our minds. Perhaps there could be other metaphiers leading to a different texture of consciousness, but in Western culture 'seeing' and the other words with which we try to anchor mental events are indeed visual. And by using this word 'see', we bring with it its paraphier, or associates of actual seeing.

In this way the spatial quality of the world around us is being driven into the psychological fact of solving a problem (which as we remember needs no consciousness). And it is this associated spatial quality that, as a result of the language we use to describe such psychological events, becomes with constant repetitions this functional space of our consciousness, or mind-space. Mind-space I regard as the primary feature of consciousness. It is the space, which you preoptively are 'introspecting on' or 'seeing' at this moment.

But who does the 'seeing'? Who does the introspecting? Here we introduce analogy, which differs from metaphor in that there the similarity is between relationships rather than between things or actions. As the body with its sense organs (referred to as I) is to physical seeing, so there develops automatically an analog 'I' to relate to this mental kind of 'seeing' in mind-space. The analog 'I' is the second most important feature of consciousness. It is not to be confused with the self, which is an object of consciousness in later development. The analog 'I' is contentless, related I think to Kant's transcendental ego. As the bodily I can move about in its environment looking at this or that, so the analog 'I' learns to 'move about' in mind-space, 'attending to' or concentrating on one thing or another.

All the procedures of consciousness are based on such metaphors and analogies with behavior, constructing a careful matrix of considerable stability. And so we narratize the analogic simulation of actual behavior, an obvious aspect of consciousness which seems to have escaped previous synchronic discussions of consciousness. Consciousness is constantly fitting things into a story, putting a before and an after around any event. This feature is an analog of our physical selves moving about

through a physical world with its spatial successiveness which becomes the successiveness of time in
mind-space. And this result in the conscious conception of time, which is a spatialized time in which
we locate events and indeed our lives. It is impossible to be conscious of time in any other way than
as a space.   <—

The universe is the
message of itself. Jaynes is not saying who we are
is who we tell ourselves we are. Who we say we are
is revealed in our telling of who we say we are. that
shows us the matter of facts.   I is the ratio
between the senses, so says McLuhan. a short skip
from the analog 'I' of Jaynes. let the record show
and tell it's sound reasoning of resonance. god bless
us. and please, let us save ourselves.

what can we say about the analog 'I'?   the
viewer arises with viewership.

McLuhan expressed very similar ideas. Julian Jaynes must have known about Marshall McLuhan but i get no hint of McLuhan influencing Jaynes. They are just saying the same thing. McLuhan also states the speed up of culture by technology created a psychic schism registered as anxiety. McLuhan does not see a God speaking to people as group think, but he does say early man was linked in aurally, where all information was shared. Myths containing the groups' wisdom were passed on in storytelling. Everyone heard the story at the same time. We were linked as a group as our attention was focused on the same bit of news at the same time. Our responses to what is heard would be occurring at the same time. We shared a tribal identity.

Books were expensive, too expensive for anyone but the rich and centers of learning until the Gutenberg press. This press with its movable type allowed for the mass production of reading material. Individuals could now afford to own books, books they can now read at the time of their own choosing in which to reflect on what has been written. The idea of the analog 'I' of Jaynes, is that this is the functioning of the mind as a house of fractal mirrors. The self or the 'I' is the act, the process of this reflection of one's thoughts, or observations, which of course would include sounds, smells, tactile sensations, our emotions and this sense of familiarity with one's self gives us the sense of a self which lasts. We have the sense of 'I' automatically and it persists through time. Julian Jaynes agrees with what Descartes is saying in essence. The self that we speak of is the self that we know of, and this self Jaynes says is largely fashioned by language.

Using language, people often mistake the word for the thing. People want to communicate something. The exact word is not important in most cases, but people make it so. So it's become a big deal if God is called Shiva, or Allah, or Buddha. Is it a coincidence that after Malaysia banned anyone but Muslims from writing the name Allah that a plane mysteriously dropped off the screen and only the frustrated rescue efforts remained of this plane? Using language has been a metaphysical challenge.

Marshall McLuhan's premise is the medium is the massage. We are like fish in the sea who do not know of water. This is how the media we use creates a medium we are within which influences us unknowingly. It molds us and we shape our minds through the medium of that act of perception. When we read, our eyes are moving along with the sentence but we have an overall view as well. Our eyes are focused on the script. This is the work of reading, to keep one's eyes focused on the subject. Similar to how Descartes speaks of the imagination, which he says takes work to put together ideas. Once the ideas get together flow happens.

Flow happens as Lao-Tzu said, a step at a time.

A central thesis in McLuhan's work is the effect reading has had. Reading encouraged people to be individuals. We could carry around our own books and think. Fantasize. Reflect. Recall. Remember. Associate. We could grow more on our own mentally. The act of reading helped build and reinforce the sense of a private self. We had our private thoughts. In Jaynes' hypothesis, the bicameral human, the person who did not self reflect, did not make their own decisions, these people did not in Jaynes' view have an interior self. They lacked the sense of 'I' that we call the self. and in Jaynes' view, this is the self that Rene Descartes described. This is the self that can think. It can remember and make things important. It is the self that can problem solve, which now that the breakdown of the bicameral mind has occurred, we no longer get instructions of what to do without our even being aware. We did not make decisions, for the decisions were always told to us. We find ourselves out of the Eden of no decisions to stress about, cast out into the chasm of modernity.

the medium is the massage. for something to feel natural, you have to forget about it. and this is how it is with ourself. We have a buoyancy to our Being. There is a peace we usually don't get to remember because we are caught and chained by time. Our lives go forward as we are run by the clock. We are run by the trains of association in the world out there. Which is how you want it, cause that way it can be quiet and peaceful inside. no time. no hassles. that's the essence. slacker heaven. then you can be as energetic as you want to be. you just have to get up to speed. You can detach from your senses and from your thoughts if you should only be so lucky. It isn't always so easy.

So most everyone on the spiritual path is looking for some peace and quiet on the inside. because that's where it's peaceful and quiet, but not if we stay there too long, because we are not peaceful. otherwise we would not be seeking peace.

It's not peaceful out here on the outside. Out here, we've lost the VOICE OF AUTHORITY for God is a question to us. It's a confused situation here in the absence of an agreed upon statement of fact. some people think the truth is other than facts. the facts speak for themselves and this is the truth.

here in the house of mirrors people take the image for the thing. They are caught in a hall of mirrors. caught up for the sake of appearance, they do not hear the voice, the inner guidance.

Antonin Scalia died yesterday, may his soul rot in hell forever. His friends Ruth and Ellen Kagen had good things to say about him. We have our private selves that must compromise in order to get along in this daily crush of contradiction. Look, I did not go to law school. But I know if I see behavior it

tells me a story. We humans, as Julian Jaynes pointed out, frame events as stories. Putting a before and
after to an event gives it a sense, a meaning. It fits
into our understanding of the flow of our lives, which
consists of awkward beginning and endings. it is not
all comfortable.

I read how Scalia used a line of reasoning
one day. Later that week he lambasted an attorney
for using that same line of reasoning. He had forgotten he used it or he could never have admonished
the other man for using that same logic. Now, we
know Scalia used his mind for his own purposes.
He had no concern about the appearance of justice when he would go on hunting trips with people
who shared a similar conservative background, and
with whom he was involved in law cases. We out
here in the open, we know it stinks. His language
was overblown to cover up his posturing. He was a
smug man. He lacked empathy. He was the little shit
who gained power and he used it. He lorded over us
and now he is dead. I only wish bad things for him.
for Ruth, you are a fool. He was an obnoxious man.
Maybe a good man to those privileged to go to the

Opera and to sit on the bench with him, but not for us who have to live in the stink of his lies. We live the obvious while you chat with the devil. Ruth, get a clue. For the sake of your own inner peace you have a compromised view of things. He butchers logic. Out here in the real world, people who work in the slaughter house can't get the stink of the offal off of us or out of our minds Ruth. so fuck you. i have to pick on my own kind.

i'm a maggotbrain with a buckethead. the story we tell ourselves is a movie. the fact of the movie is a question. the question concerns why we are here and is this necessary. as i see it, the universe is an ongoing fact which includes you and where you are located physically. this universe, it has little concern with how you feel about it. thus we get Schopenhauer seeing the World as a mad force, a mindless uncontrolled torrential outpouring, an unceasing never ending madness which he thought it would be wise to tame by seeking serenity in art. a pacification via buddhism. He selects images of peace to counter what he sees as the truth of this world. but this world is not how he sees it. as bad as it is, the worst problem is, it is so boring. so devoid of truth. A world in which Clarence Thomas sits on the bench is not a world free of sensing the absurd. buffoonery at the Highest Level. Our crap idea of Justice. It's not justice when Clarence Thomas is on the bench. Someone is lying and my money is on Clarence, or the woman who says Clarence lied is lying. so someone is lying. and my money is on Clarence. So what are we doing with our lives in the mean time, here at the masquerade?

good news: 2/14/2016 11:38 AM I found out this morning thru Calvin, that Julio saw Lee assault me. I am thinking Lee can get arrested for assault! I emailed my lawyer and should hear back tomorrow. otherwise I would go to the sheriff today.

6:41 PM. read Religion by Schopenhauer today. very enjoyable. He is a witty and funny fellow. Previously I wrote about Schopenhauer based on things I read and watched about Schopenhauer. Since then I listened to a reading of his, "Studies in Pessimism", and this today. I am of the belief if someone is depressed, they should listen to Schopenhauer, for all his remarks about the artifice and petty nature of people are so true. To hear these truths is an antidote for those of us who have to suffer the reality of what he says, but he can take a step farther and see what I see.

In Religion he says something very good, "But the difficulty is to teach the multitude that something can be both true and untrue at the same time." He says people don't recognize an allegory contains a spiritual truth but is not totally true. What he writes in 1850 is as true today, how people miss the spirit by thinking and convincing themselves of their beliefs by their beliefs. Religions have been one of the major forces driving wars and hatred.

Arthur says the idea of reincarnation is more rational to explain man's bad luck than God as creator. He finds the Jewish image of God to be not so good as an explanation. It is not his cup of tea.

He makes a factual mistake in saying the Jews do not believe in reincarnation. Actually, reincarnation is a belief Jews historically have held. His logical mistake is to see a difference where there is none, and if there is, the God as creator, with it's Adam and Eve version has its advantages. Arthur demonstrates his consciousness is conscious of his rhetorical argument, not of the actual facts, as Julian Jaynes has pointed out for us. And Arthur's argument is with the Protestant idea that a soul could be predestined to spend an eternity in hell, more than with the Jews who he says are from made from a tree trunk of alien growth.

Schopenhauer says reincarnation makes more sense to describe conditions here on earth than the idea God made something out of nothing. He thinks it is cruel and inhuman for God to have created the conditions humans find themselves in. Better if we blame ourselves, as is the idea in reincarnation.. We deserve what we get because of past sins. Sort of like Adam and Eve, except it's your fault for something you did in a past life, which you believe you had. In either case the person's condition is explained in terms of previous bad behavior, an inability to follow instructions, done by someone with a different body than yours. Schopenhauer is seeing a difference where there is no difference, and he thinks one view is superior.

My idea of philosophy is to make a recipe or to state the possibility for happiness. The goal of life according to Ramana Maharshi is to be happy. It's to know God, but that's an idea in a way. God is real, yet God turns into an idea if we think about it and set it as a goal. The idea of God makes it foreign to us and allows us to feel guilt as if we are somehow lacking. It is our fault if we are not aware of God is the view reinforced by most religions. However, we are not living in a vacuum. God as an idea has a reality to it and can be seen as a goal without creating a paradoxical obstacle.

In order to be happy there must be an actual possibility for happiness. What is the quality of the Jews that Schopenhauer finds so awful? Why does Arthur say we Jews are from alien stock? He says, "the fundamental characteristics of the Jewish religion are realism and optimism."

So, what's Buddhism and the religion of the Brahmans got going for them that Schopenhauer finds more appealing? "Idealism and pessimism."

This is superior to the realism and optimism of the Jews, who he says, treat this world as "absolutely real", while Buddhism and the religion of Brahman look at this world as a dream in which our pain is a result of our past sins

Now, despite the fact Schopenhauer said we Jews are from alien stock, he says the Jewish religion springs from Zoroastrianism, which he calls Zendavesta. He uses terms which seem they've got a Gnostic twist to them.

There are similarities to be seen between Judaism and Zoroastrianism. Both have uncertain dates of their origin, somewhere in the ballpark of 1400-1800 BCE give or take a bunch of centuries. Some stories have Zoroaster, or Zarathusthra, as he is known living around 800 BCE, yet Judaism is as old as that, so if Judaism springs from the religion of Zarathustra, he must have lived earlier. Their founders have similar stories. Both stories have a worked out biography. Abraham, whose father dealt idols for a living had the intuition these idols are not the real thing. His inkling shares certain respects with the awakening of Ramana Maharshi, an intuition of the underlying reality. Zarathustra was a priest in his religion but was visited by the spirit Good Thought on behalf of the god Ahuramazda saying it's time to do away with animal sacrifices, that and we should have good reflection, good thoughts, and good deeds. It is a faith which says we are responsible for our actions.

Abraham shepherd sheep out of Ur, Babylonia. Zarathustra kept his camel in Bactria, a hump or two away, as the caravan travels. Now why would Mr. Schopenhauer say the Jews are so wrong for being optimistic and realistic in our religion, yet our religion comes from the religion of, how he puts it, Zendavesta? Because Mr. Schopenhauer is very upset that in the Bible, God created the world out of nothing and called it good. Just like that. God did the deed, swept his hands, called it good and was done for the day. Do you see a problem? As I see it, if a God created a universe and called it good, that God must have thought it good. So where's the problem? The problem is Arthur suffers from a syndrome of errors..

His fundamental error is to make a system which was not as God put it, "all good," but must account for evil to explain the reason for our pessimism. Schopenhauer is upset that the Jews in their allegory do not place evil up there with God.

What if we didn't have to account for evil? If all is good, we can handle the devil in the details.

If all is good as pronounced by God is true, happiness is possible here. Satan only has a subordinate position in Judaism. This is why Arthur is upset. The bible does not explain evil in good enough detail for him.

Zoroastrianism gives a prominent place to Evil. The forces of darkness led by the Spiritual Enemy, Ahriman duke it out with the forces of light led by Ahuramazda to give the world a four-stage cycle, much like exists in Hinduism. Schopenhauer remarks that the god in Zoroastrianism, Ahruramazda who he calls Ormuzd is in fact a transformation of the Hindu god, Indra. Zarathustra and his father were priests in the worship of Mithra, which bears similarities to the religion next door in India. The holy text of the Zoroastrians is the Avesta. The Avesta uses similar terms for spirits and demons as the Rig Veda of Hinduism, which might date the Avesta at 1400 BCE.

The problem for Arthur lies in the fact that the two doctrines of the Old and the New Testament are combined in the Christian religion. He feels the two systems are incompatible. It's an allegory giving rise to absurdities which was completed by Augustine. Injury was added to insult by Luther. What is absurd and revolting writes Arthur, is that in the Jewish Bible mankind was created by an outside will. God created something out of nothing. We were called into existence and here we are. It is true he writes, that morality is innate, yet more rational than innate morality he writes, is the idea of reincarnation where if we don't get it at first, we can keep on repeating our mistakes.

The answer for Arthur lies in the Avatar, a clearly Indian idea. From Indra he expects. I see the logical point Schopenhauer is driving to. If the God of the Jews proclaimed, "All is good" why would we need a messiah to appear as prophesied in the Bible?   so bring up an avatar as an imported idea.

So much better for Schopenhauer if this world were but a stepping-stone for what lies beyond. The Jews found happiness here, happy with material comforts. Resignation in this world is his philosophical prescription.

something from nothing is his complaint. form as emptiness, emptiness as form is his argument. Forgotten in his rhetoric is God's communication from Abraham to Zarathustra. Joy is known through revelation, not pessimism.

Schopenhauer neglected to mention the agreement God made with Abraham in his discussion of religion. The fact we still have God's guidance is the story of the Bible. Schopenhauer saw it from his perspective, which demonstrates the insight of Julian Jaynes. We are wrapped up in our thought bubble as a private aquarium in which we view the world.

the ongoing agreement is my understanding of salvation. the coolest path might be advaita, as a means of understanding, but if you want to complete your path, become a siddha. for the siddhas are always already siddhas. you are always you and you are the meditation. God never left.

there is not a higher and a lower in god. there is no need in the undifferentiated to say this is this and that is that. but here in this world we certainly do. there are specific deeds to be done at certain times. fuzzy wuzzy doesn't cut when a sling blade can.

The Bible as seem from the perspective of Julian Jaynes and the bicameral mind is a manual for God to insert itself in us as us. God is the understanding. the completion. the goal of nirvana. done by being itself, otherwise known as reality.

God is the only occupant here. All creatures large and small are God. All sensations, all sounds, colors, shapes and sizes are God. anything and everything you can think of is God. In fact, it all happens to be God. this is the perspective as seem from God. is there a problem here?

because if there is, listen for the voice of guidance. the voice shows up from time to time within our lives. we've all got it, no matter who we think we are.

for God, there is no problem. God is the whole. the universe is the message of itself. it is self explicit.

2/16/2016 12:28 PM. not having heard from the lawyer, I went to the West Hollywood Sheriffs and filed a complaint about Lee. I was told the police report will be available in ten days.

2/17 7:22 AM. to understand Advaita Vedanta is to be a siddha. the true teaching of advaita is all is Brahman. All is the great expanse of this universe. Everywhere is expansiveness. The nature of everything is Brahman. All that exists is always and only Brahman. All that exists is realization. Anything and everything that exists is realization. Nothing is apart from God. There is nothing to know. There is nothing to realize, for you are that before you realize it. to be yourself is to be a siddha.

you can not practice this yoga. this yoga blows your mind.

the source of evil is the poser, the great pretender who is born out of fear which gives birth to the struggle for power. This is the Evil who is our plague, those who act without understanding.

In Advaita Vedanta, All is Brahman, All is God. there are no emanations, no gradations, no levels and degrees of what is so. God is God and God is Absolutely Real. This too is That. This is not a dress rehearsal. This is not a stage on the way to somewhere, this is it. If you surrender your little mind into who you already are; that which you are already, the bigger you, who does not have a problem, is not plagued by evil, who does not need an explanation.

we came naked and naked we will go. now i am, and tho i wear clothes, i am naked inside. there is nobody home, only God. only the wisdom i hear from the only voice which pays attention. God speaks thru us all. whoever speaks the truth is speaking of what is and God is not separate from what is. there is nowhere to look, there is nowhere to go where God is not, because God is everything all the time. so, obviously if there is a problem, it lies with us. There is no sin. Naked i came into this world. my mind consists of perceptions and the paths which describe them.

we suffer the sin of origanalism. it's uniquely american, like jazz, chiropractic, and sunflowers.

there is no going back to an original nirvana to reach perfection. In the beginning slavery was legal in this country. Our constitution was signed on September 17, 1787. In 1791 the Bill of Rights was signed. Our country was not of one mind. Our constitution did not speak for everyone. Not everyone was pleased. The anti-federalists were worried the federal government might take away individual liberties, so ten amendments were added.

The irony of poor thinkers like Clarence Thomas who espouses such a closed minded view is pathetic. Most of the activity of the thinking of Thomas and Scalia is to not grant individuals freedom. To not adapt with the time and to improve, but to keep things how our founding fathers wanted it. But our founding fathers were not in agreement. Changes were needed and made after four years and have continued.

If our founding fathers knew changes had to be made and made them, how can someone keep a fantasy going that things were so peachy to begin with that the best idea for justice is to stay there? Stay in fantasyland, a land that never was. a land which exists in their imagination only. it is a fiction, it is the idealism of which Schopenhauer speaks as being opposite of being realistic and finding solutions in this world; This world where we find ourselves.

Fantasyland, the wish to go back to an original nirvana, a land of peace and quiet, law and order, bliss and satisfaction, depth and comfort of the non-self who is not troubled by actual circumstances, does not exist. There is an all-encompassing existence in which we exist. Our aim is not to go back to our mommy's womb.

Scalia and Thomas do not understand human nature. They lack an empathetic intelligence. Their thoughts are derived from their beliefs, not honesty. Clarence Thomas is a perjurer who does not belong on the Supreme Court.

People think they know themselves, but the idea people have of who they are can turn in a second to what is feared. People who espouse ideals as the goal are in league with that desire which is a wish. People are not who they think they are. Time and time again, we see this world we thought civilized is not so. Countries like Great Britain and Belgium were guilty of horrible atrocities in their efforts to control wealth and power..

Schopenhauer is an idiot. He loved to call people names. It makes him so amusing and often right, but his essential message is so wrong. He totally misses the point of the Buddhist scriptures and the Upanishads he held in such high esteem. The Buddhist scriptures are about the illusion of one's self. If one's self is an illusion, to whom is the world going to appear to be an awful place? Hume understood the Buddhist breakthrough; there is no self. Schopenhauer didn't get it. And the Upanishads? The Upanishads are Yogic. They speak of the all encompassing and totally transcending nature of Brahman being the soul reality. The message of yoga is the atman and Brahman are one. The essence of you and the nature of Reality are not contiguous, they are identical. The Upanishads and the Vedas are all about God. the crown jewel of the Vedas is Advaita Vedanta. not-two.

but we live here in the land of the tick-tock. the cuckoo and the mockingbird; a copy and its mimic.

"the word is not the thing."
~ Alfred Korzybski 1933

We take words to be the gospel. If a password is needed, if lyrics are to be sung, sure. but in general words signify something and are not the thing in itself. When it comes to education, words are usually the objects played with in our minds. If the class is music, math, gym, art, etc., words are an aid to what we are out to achieve, not the thing in itself. When it comes to information, words are much of the environment. There are visual images, graphs, charts, and sounds to aid us, but the word is the thing and in that activity the word presents its two-fold nature. It can be real and it can be taken to be real.

this is the source of evil. deception arises out of confusion. if we start off with bad directions, it takes time to recover.

What is the thing in itself? for me, it is what's behind the present activity. Our present activity speaks of what it is. It is not something else. It is not an unknowable aspect of ourselves which is needed in order to be a completed spiritual being. For me, it is the simple feel of the thing. the taste, the sound, the sensation, the recognition.

Awareness is special. It happens when it happens and at no other time. Catch it when you can. For me, the idea of siddha means completion. There is a knowing which means this thing can be ongoing. Completion means an understanding. With that, we can let the thing run itself.

but people take the slogan for the under-standing. people get sold on what to believe. this is a form of slavery to our own mind. liberation is to have your own mind, and as Hume knew, there is no one there inside to claim the prize of being the self. there is no self that we could call our self, and yet, we are the self. We are something made of nothing.

to be liberated is to be free of time.　the thing in itself is just what we are doing, even if that is nothing much, just existing. to be free of what bound us, so we are free to be doing what we are doing. that is liberation.

All creatures have an awareness and all creatures identify as themselves, immunologically, as they are aware. Julian Jaynes says the 'I' springs automatically. 'I' is a feature of consciousness. I believe the bicameral man who Jaynes spoke of, the person who existed before the breakdown of the bicameral mind, those who still heard the voice of their god through the right hemisphere, they would have an awareness of themselves as existing and as being themselves. They would be the person who felt pain or pleasure; they just did not dwell in their thoughts. the voice they paid attention to as far as rumination goes, would be the voice of the god who told them what to think deeply about, what to concern themselves with.

Jaynes says that consciousness is not perception. Consciousness as he uses it, is the inner Cartesian Theatre of Our Mind. It is the inner soul, the place where we dwell and ruminate. It is the place where we live.

For a dog to eat food, the dog knows it is eating. but when the food is gone, it is gone. Now, dogs are very aware. They have insight. They look forward to the next bite. They are well aware of schedules. They know the prompts to get things happening. and they relive. dogs have memories. Dogs dream. what they dream, i do not know, but i know they dream. i imagine a dog dream is going on in the dog's mind, but like Hume says, the 'I' which we take as real, is not really real. We are like Time. We do not exist as an actual thing. We are not a substance. We are the whole thing, but to speak of us as us, we are the recognition of ourselves. We signify ourselves as ourselves and in this way, as Jaynes says, consciousness is based on language.

Creatures might not have an inner dialogue creating a self, but they are aware. Our bodies have an awareness of what they do without our being aware. The awareness of the body is not much different than how we experience our body. We can chew, swallow, speak, and breathe. Our minds easily slide from what they are aware of to the next thing. We drop off our previous contemplation without thinking about it. Once in a while we take note of something and think we are aware. I find perception and consciousness to be one thing. Our consciousness might be the gleaning of our sense data. We are living the tip of the iceberg.

The job of the mind is to identify things, to name them. That way it knows what it is doing and can go on about its business. Our mind takes the identification of something, its name, to indicate. Identification is not knowing in terms of building blocks, of how this is put together. It does not contain the full history of that subject. No, its identity is established and can be built on. To know does not mean to be all knowing. To know is to know when to look and see.

Thinking and knowing is hard. In an evolutionary sense, thinking is part of the package. To think is to adapt. To give the right answer is to get rewarded. To be in a system, one must give the right answer, even if it is wrong, so it pays to be dumb. This is a problem. It is the problem of belief. People who don't know instruct others. It is the blind leading the blind. The effects have been catastrophic.

To be really comfortable is to master a subject. Mastering a subject means you know. You are the authority. You do not need help in general, but if you did, you would know to ask. To be a Master is to not look over the shoulder in fear that we may be wrong. A true religion would have us not looking over our shoulder in fear. There cannot be a God hiding behind us unseen, waiting. We have to be one with God or we will never be in peace. to be at one means we are one.

to be a spiritual communist is to surrender your small self. it is to have no ownership of a soul. i do not have a separate existence. there is no me in the real sense. we only exist as an image in a house of mirrors. our name is our dog tag, needed strictly for identification purposes.

You are held together by your memories. Your memories and your thinking makes you who you are. Thinking arises out of sensing and movement. It is the interplay of feedback. As we fall asleep, our memories are loosened. Who we are is let go and we exist. We are. We are that which we are, something unspeakable.

We are awareness. That's who we are. Thinking is a function of awareness. Thinking is an activity. It is a circling.

Evil is simply getting the names wrong. to insist on it. to make it a point and to convince others.

To exist in time is to court anxiety. Creatures do not like anxiety and will instinctively do what it takes to stay clear of that predicament. So crowd control in the form of peer pressure makes us conform during our formative years and as adults. To live in a system is to be a subject of that system. The system supplies the correct answer. So in America, we have American answers, in Russia, they have Russian answers.

The political system along with religion has replaced the bicameral voice of God to tell us what is the right thing to do without the need to think about it. To exist as a human involves a bit of indoctrination. Thinking is done in order to not think. This is true whether someone is a Master or a Slave. Systems are large and operate with an intelligence of their own.

To buy into the belief of a system is to be free of anxiety. but if the system's belief system is a mythology, this is only a temporary numbing of the anxiety.

Germany went through a period of psychosis. Italy and Japan joined in and they took on the world. So much of Europe was destroyed. Millions of Jews and other unwanted people were sent to concentration camps. The fire bombings of Tokyo were as bad as the two atom bombs that went off, as all of war is bad, not just what we talk about. The world is like a Phoenix. World War II, a war unlike any other in how totally devastating were the results. and the war in Afghanistan and Iraq drags on longer than World War II.

George W. Bush belongs in prison.

George W. Bush is evil. He had a talk with God and from that conversation led us into a war with Iraq, which distracted us. and we haven't completed a thing. George is a slogan monger who belongs in jail. George W. Bush looked into Vladimir Putin's eyes and says he saw his soul. George lies.

George has an idea of what is good and holy. He wants to say and do the right thing but he has no understanding. He has made a terrible mess. Bush, who ridiculed the idea of nation building tried to force democracy on Iraq. The lack of any understanding is so astounding. George W. Bush belongs in jail.

In the films of Hitler, the Germans look really into it. People like being mindless robots or an army of ants. Maybe Julian Jaynes was right. I don't think he is telling all of the story. I think animals are aware, plants are aware, and there have always been people who are aware of the awareness in themselves and others. There have always been people who are gifted in a psychic sense. I would think the discovery of alcohol helped get the party going, loosened people's lips and they found a way to talk about it. and psychedelics.

George W. Bush is a deceived man as is much of the Republican Party. They take what they hope and believe to be true to be true. They believe the appearance of reality rather than to be grounded in reality and to have honesty in their thinking. George is a dishonest man. He lied and got us into a war we did not need. The man belongs in jail.

Evil is to worship at the altar of Platonic Idolatry, that there is an external reality as a key to wisdom. but in truth, there is no evil, which has a reality of its own. It is part and parcel of how we describe this to ourselves. We have the word evil. There is evil, but what is evil changes. There is not a force of evil, which battles God. That is mythology.

The mind makes a now by superimposing different views into one view. it takes what it is looking at and merges the looking into what it sees. the mind selects and focuses in on that. It jumps from one view to the next and weaves it into a seamless viewing. The mind sees in wholes. it focuses in on one area, but it sees as a whole. And so, the person thinks they are seeing the whole. They see the whole their mind sees as it jumps from image to image. This is identified. That is identified. It puts a before and an after with each view as that is sliced into the overall previous view so we live our lives in a contiguous manner. we fashion our life segmentally. this is what it means to be an evolutionary being. we worm up.

the mind takes what it sees to be the whole, but it negates that fact of itself when the mind thinks it is seeing the whole. It is standing outside of the whole not knowing it is included in it. The mind, composed of time, gives the appearance of existing at a certain time within time, but it is composing the view it sees. Since we agree we exist in time as our eyeballs pull our attention this way or that, or the thought of something jumps us onto another train of thought, we exist as a thing within that which is not a thing. It contains and metabolizes. It's more than what the mind can think of, because the mind can exist in a state in which it does not think; yet it is every bit as aware as those who are busy thinking.

Our psyche is a house. We live on a planet but we live in houses. in apartments, in shelters, in dwellings.

People, animals, plants, things, which are alive want to be so. They want to continue. There is a drive towards balance. Within a system the tendency is for things to settle into place. That's what it is to have a system. The parts of the system, the citizens, they all have an inherent tendency to protect the system, to keep up their role. In jnana yoga, the vrittis or vasanas; our habits, are that which keep one in bondage. Karma is bad, as the individual acts are the ones that count, but our habits keep us doing the same things over again and again. More subtle is the habit we have of being our selves. That too is something, which is a balance, a harmony of the composites of so many images. We find through experience how we are. We have an essential self, but we know ourselves thru time.

The idea of a separate self is ingrained in us. We have been indoctrinated into a system of belief. Our beliefs might be a reaction to the belief we grew up in, but it is a belief non-the less.

As creatures in time who do not have access to all the information available. we have our concerns. We want things to be alright. We don't want people upsetting the apple cart, so there is a tendency to distrust. And for good reasons. It is the job of the mind to take care of who it is with. To go beyond our self we have to surrender our mind, as our mind holds the conceptual limits of how we perceive. To go beyond one's self is a form of ego death, and the mind is programmed to protect, so the timing must be right to surrender one's self.

To transcend must be done in cooperation with the mind. We exist in a state of unknowing. Information, which turns into knowledge and wisdom, is the stuff which runs the projector in the inner Cartesian Theatre of the Mind. Therefor, information is crucial. Therefor information is the gospel; it is what we fight about. What is right and what is wrong. Our lives and our opinions of ourselves depend on it.

Why does truth matter? Because if something is poison it can kill you, so it's best to be aware. In nature, organisms have learned mimicry. plants or animals may look alike, but one might be poisonous and the other not. What is poisonous to one species is tolerable to another. So, if an animal learns something is okay to eat, that is valuable information.

Whatever system we live in is like the conditions Julian Jaynes describes in The Origin of Consciousness in the Breakdown of the Bicameral Mind. Those at the top have the voice of authority. Once orders are given there is a certain amount of following the orders without thinking about it. Orders are to be carried out, not thought about. Time is of the essence and we do not have time to think when the order has been given. So we act without delay.

Which is good and necessary. We learn things which we incorporate into ourselves. In that way, we ourselves are like the voice of God. We tell ourselves what to do as we are learning a new skill, like playing the violin. Some passages are faster than the mind can read. The body must learn the notes and play in a learned, remembered way. It is automatic through learning. It is a cooperative effort of folding one's mind into one's activity.

The ego is the time for self-reflection. It is a time for learning. It is the training wheel level of life. It is wonderful and it is essential. It is the inner soul of the being, the creature with a body, or the creature who is a body. We will always have our inner self, our inner animal who needs attending. So, we will always have our ego. But an ego is a thing which has its time and space of necessity. It has become the predominant way that humans know themselves. We are stuck in a childhood fascination with ourselves.

There is a paradox, a catch-22. There is only one being here, and it is a conspiracy to keep ourselves at the level of the ego. the Catch-22 is, if the other ego has not surrendered their ego, it is not safe to surrender ours, and to transcend the ego is best done as a cooperative effort. If another has not surrendered the ego, it is not safe. Since it is the mind's job to protect the body, if there is danger from another ego, the mind instinctively knows not to surrender the ego, the protective mechanisms. And so, people have forgot what it is to be ego free.

The system works by peer pressure. We work as guards to keep one another in place. The crime people have fallen prey to is to believe the word is the thing.

Whoever invented Christianity got it all wrong. Whatever Adam + Eve did in the Garden of Eden has very little to do with Judaism. Judaism is not about making amends for the original sin. Judaism is a different religion with a different mind set than Christianity. The Christian and Buddhist doctrines paint existence as the wrong place to be. God did us wrong, if there is a God. I might have written a proof that God exists. In doing so, I convinced myself the soul exists. The idea of mysticism is to transcend the idea of a separate self, so if we do have a soul, that is the thing that spiritual seekers have been attempting to get rid of, or to see the timelessness in it. But if we see the timelessness in our soul, we transcend our individual existence. There are multiple orders of infinities, but there is truly only one timeless region or zone called Eternity. that is who and what God is. That which transcends.

The thing which runs the universe runs us, who are in this universe. That thing and you are not different things. You are the whole. We know ourselves as ourselves, but we are more than we could ever know.

If you could know all of this, it would take so much time, i do not think you would really want to bother. but if you do, knock yourself out thinking this is about knowing stuff. I don't think it is. There is too much to know. better to know some things which you are attracted to and want to know.

When people do not know what they are doing they make mistakes. Too much or too little force is used. Most often when it comes to authority, too much force is used.

People want to learn. just not what we are forced to be taught. people detect fakery, but as there is no alternative, we become fakes ourselves. Descartes might have proved it to me and to himself that this is real, but we forget. we are made to forget and to rest. but if something isn't right we do not get to rest.

The word is not the thing. Isn't it obvious who knows what they are talking about and who is repeating a lesson to be studied or remembered? What animates us? what draws our interest and our attention?

People want to do the right thing. in general. even the bad people, they think they are doing right by doing wrong, otherwise why would they be doing it? they think it is their right. the problem with people is the matter that Schopenhauer writes about. The will. our willfulness.

the ten ox herding pictures of Zen. our nature is not different than us. to see our nature as some-thing different is to see the spiritual path as something which is needed in order to calm or quell our spirit. but our spirit is not something different than us. in the ten ox herding pictures of Zen, drawings were done to describe the adventure. A boy is given an ox to take care of. the ox is the representation of the world. it is a beast. it is strong and perhaps difficult to tame. the methods people have used to tame the beast have been matters of discipline and control, enforced hours of meditation, of diets, of asceticism, of study, all types of techniques.

none were needed. earlier versions of the ten pictures only had six. the boy recognized this ox was given to him by the Zen master to attain a break thru, satori, and the boy recognized his nature is the nature of the ox, which made any discipline unnecessary, for this was a conversation between the boy and himself. and so he realized satori, everlasting satori. like a breath of sunlight.

ABOUT THE AUTHOR

Howard Venze began the practice of yoga at a young age. Inspired by spiritual literature, novels and Mad Magazine, Howard formed the idea he wanted to get enlightened while a teenager. He figured having a teacher was the way for him. He reached that goal in 1992 while meditating with the spiritual teacher Leslie Temple Thurston. Howard has worked as a chiropractor and a nurse. After retiring from nursing, Venze has written two books, meditates often and is developing an effortless yoga, safe for geezers.

WWW.HOWARDVENZE.COM

From FLUID LUHANCY PRESS

In his book *Onomatopoetic Massage*, Howard takes us on a metaphysical journey. Continuing the path taken by physics from the time of Newton to the conceptual space-time of Einsten, Howard gets to the root of definitions and demolishes the idea of time as actuality and resurrects both time and Maya (bondage) as the activity of our life measured. To flip the gestalt of our scientific revolution, our paradigm concerning God's creation is in it's original formation there was no problem, the truth is we are free, not bound to start with. Life is a journey of discovery not from ignorance to enlightenment but from this to that. Howard argues both Jesus and the Buddha had it wrong. You know more than they did, You have it more together than they did, until the authority of what is right instructed us on right and wrong. We as living Beings are agents of change. It's now or never in Howard's mind. There is no time but the present which is fleeting, so look within these pages where the distinction between in and out, this and that are confused.

ONOMATOPOETIC
MASSAGE
a metaphysical primer
HOWARD
VENZE

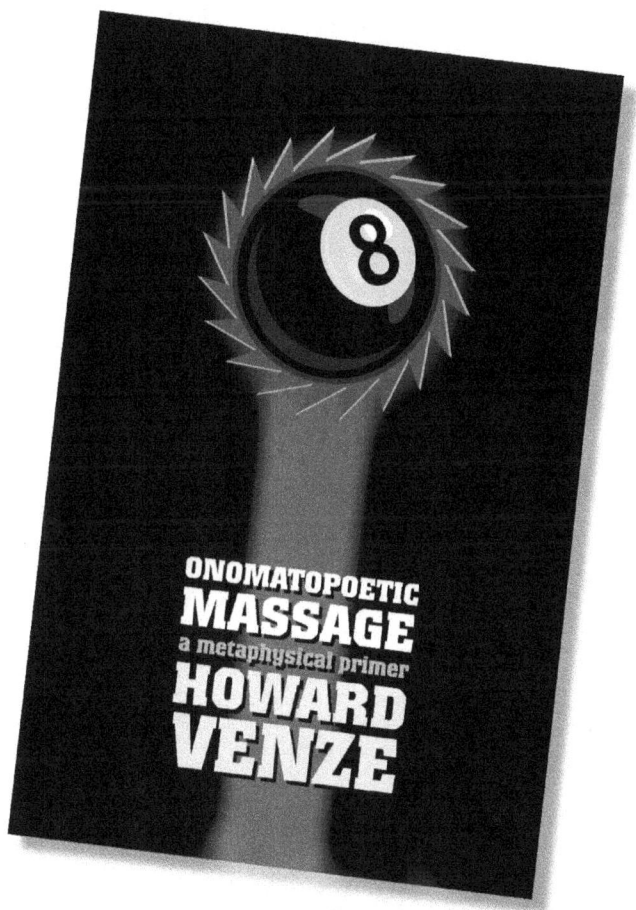

THE EXCITING NEW MEMOIR BY
AMERICA'S MAD METAPHYSICIAN

ONOMATOPOETIC
MASSAGE
a metaphysical primer
HOWARD
VENZE

Available Online at **BARNES&NOBLE**
BN.com

It's About Time

HOWARD VENZE

FLUID LUXANCY PRESS · FLUID LUXANCY PRESS · FLUID LUXANCY PRESS · FLUID LUXANCY PRESS